CONSERVATIVE
REVOLUTION

CONSERVATIVE REVOLUTION

THE CENTRE FOR POLICY STUDIES AT 50

First published in 2024 by
The Centre for Policy Studies

Copyright © The Centre for Policy Studies, 2024

https://www.cps.org.uk

HB 978-1-914008-48-1

Project management by Whitefox
Designed by seagulls.net
Adapted and typeset by Typo•glyphix
Cover design by Tom Cabot/ketchup

Printed and bound in Great Britain by CPI Group (UK) Ltd, Croydon CR0 4YY

Contents

Introduction:
A Conservative Revolution?

ROBERT COLVILE

'The Centre for Policy Studies was where our Conservative revolution began.' That phrase, from which this book takes its title, forms the first line of Margaret Thatcher's speaking notes for her address to the think tank's AGM in 1991, less than a year after being forced out of Downing Street.[1]

She went on to list the core principles upon which she and her friend Keith Joseph had founded the CPS, and which remained at the heart of its mission: to promote 'financial orthodoxy and free enterprise', 'control government spending and borrowing', 'cut taxes, regulation and bureaucracy', 'strong defence', 'fight for free trade', 'respect nationhood' and so on.

Lady Thatcher had many more things to say about the CPS over the years. Even before she became Prime Minister, she credited it with helping her to accomplish 'the revival of the philosophy and principles of a free society' – adding that 'history will accord a very great place to Keith Joseph' for his role in that.[2]

After Joseph's death, she would argue that 'it was by implementing the policies worked out by Keith Joseph and the Centre that we gradually restored the confidence and reputation of our country once again' – an accomplishment built upon 'liberating the genius of the people and limiting the powers and role of government'.[3]

Introduction

This year, the Centre for Policy Studies is marking its 50th anniversary – a full half-century since Joseph, Thatcher, Alfred Sherman, Nigel Vinson and their allies began their remarkable crusade to transform the Conservative Party, and British society.

In many ways, it can be hard to appreciate the full scope of their success in building the capital-owning democracy of which they dreamed – precisely because they were so successful. To us it now seems commonplace that companies should be run by their executives and shareholders rather than the trade unions. That inflation is managed via monetary rather than fiscal policy. That the state should not own and operate haulage firms, travel agents or telephone lines. That money can flow freely into and out of the country. Or that you can take your pension with you when you leave your job. But all of those facts had to be argued for, and fought for.

The work of the CPS is about more than those early years – much more. If that were not so, it would not have survived over the following decades, let alone remain one of the most influential think tanks in Westminster. As Charles Moore says in our conversation later in this book, one of the crucial tasks of the CPS is to renew itself for each generation. And many of the essays here set out how it has done that, under a succession of Directors and Chairmen who have done credit to Lady Thatcher and Keith Joseph's memory, by developing policies that have done the nation a very great deal of good.

But it is fair to say, as its Director, that the legacy of those early years is both an inspiration and a rather terrifying challenge. Even as I type these words, I have only to turn in my chair to see Lady Thatcher staring sternly down from the portrait that hangs behind my desk.

Yet Lady Thatcher, I am fairly certain, would not have wanted a book such as this to be just a collection of platitudes and obsequies. And that is why we have chosen that phrase, 'Conservative revolution', as the title of this collection. Because it speaks to a tension that many of the authors here explore.

Were the accomplishments of Margaret Thatcher, and the ideology of the Centre for Policy Studies, revolutionary in spirit, as well as effect? Isn't a 'Conservative revolution' a contradiction in terms?

If so, it was a contradiction Thatcher herself was alive to. In 1996, when she delivered the inaugural Keith Joseph Memorial Lecture – reprinted here – she insisted that 'when Keith and I were struggling to shift Britain back from the socialist state, we were also acting as conservatives, with a small "c". We were seeking to re-establish an understanding of the fundamental truths which had made Western life, British life, and the life of the English-speaking peoples what they were. This was the foundation of our Conservative revolution. It remains the foundation for any successful Conservative programme of government.'

Thatcher saw her revolution, in other words, as a turning of the wheel – a restoration of a classical liberal society in which individuals are free to flourish, which in turn enables the nation to flourish with them. Dominic Sandbrook, in his essay on Thatcherism, shows that, at least in her early years, Thatcher was as eager to present herself as a traditionalist as a radical, and that her beliefs were the product as much of her biography as her ideology.

Likewise, Tim Congdon describes how monetarism, viewed by many as a dangerous innovation, was conceived by its advocates as a return to the classical liberal tradition, in the face of an economic establishment that had fallen into delusion. And of course, when making her famous claim that there was 'no such thing as society', Thatcher's point was not to assert some radical, atomised vision of human life but to point out that society was ultimately made up of individuals and families, and that they should not look constantly to government to solve their own problems.[4]

But the essays here also grapple with the tension between being conservative and revolutionary. In our conversation, Lord Moore – the Iron Lady's authorised biographer – highlights the extent to which what made her remarkable was not just her ideology, but her ability to translate that ideology into the realm of practical politics, through all the necessary compromises that brought. Charlotte Howell's essay on Alfred Sherman, the extraordinary figure who served as the CPS's first Director, shows the strain this created between the insurgents and the establishment – a story that has frequently repeated itself within the Conservative Party.

This, again, was a tension the CPS's founders were well aware of. The Centre was launched with a series of extraordinary speeches from Keith Joseph, setting out a detailed and compelling prospectus for where both Conservatives and Labour had gone wrong in the post-war years. He accompanied this by endless further lectures, in particular at universities, to evangelise his cause. (David Willetts describes in his essay the excitement of attending such an event.)

Yet what made the CPS different from existing think tanks was that it was not meant to be about ideology, but results. In its founding prospectus, there is a stern injunction that 'the purpose of the Centre will be practicable. There will be no attempt to propose policies such as denationalisation that are not politically feasible.'[5] This is a principle we have tried to adhere to during my time as Director: the way I often put it is that the function of the CPS is not merely to tell people about the delights that await them in the Promised Land, but to draw them a map to actually get there.

This is the spirit, of course, which animated the famous 'Stepping Stones' paper produced by John Hoskyns and Norman Strauss, and mentioned by multiple contributors to this collection. The paper is emblematic not just because it examined the causes of Britain's economic dysfunction – rightly concluding that there was no way to fix the situation without taking on the unions – but because it also set out the need to convince the public of that argument, in order to actually bring about the changes that the country so desperately needed.

This essay collection, then, is not a backward-looking affair. Indeed, many of its authors draw the parallels between 1974 and 2024, arguing (implicitly or explicitly) that we need a similar Conservative revolution today.

In these pages you will find Anthony Seldon writing on the CPS's early days; and Ryan Bourne on whether Thatcher's economic reforms were – to echo Alfred Sherman – just an 'interlude' between periods of swollen-state stagnation. Graham Brady reminds us that the CPS was set up to champion liberty, not just prosperity. David Willetts, Stephen Parkinson and Tim Knox explore the CPS's story after the Thatcher years, and their own time there. Alys Denby marks the 10th anniversary of CapX – the CPS's media arm, set up to continue the work of communication and evangelisation started by Joseph. Niall Ferguson, Paul Goodman, Rachel Wolf and Maurice Saatchi address, in very different ways, the connections between past and present, and the tasks that lie ahead of the CPS, and the wider Conservative movement, in the future.

I am hugely grateful to all those who contributed to this essay collection, and to all those who have worked for, written for, supported and championed the CPS over the years. I am especially grateful to my colleague Karl Williams, who has worked with me to shape and edit this book.

In her notes for that speech in 1991, Thatcher concluded by warning her friends at the CPS that the great temptation in politics was to 'lose sight of the eternal truths and choose the popular, quick fix'. It is a temptation which the CPS has spent 50 years trying to avoid. I very much hope that our successors are able to say the same 50 years hence.

Robert Colvile is Director of the Centre for Policy Studies and Editor-in-Chief of CapX.

1 Margaret Thatcher and the Centre for Policy Studies

CHARLES MOORE
in conversation with ROBERT COLVILE

Robert Colvile: When it comes to Margaret Thatcher and the Centre for Policy Studies, there are few people with greater knowledge than Lord Moore of Etchingham, one of our greatest journalists and Lady Thatcher's authorised biographer.

Charles, let me start with a couple of big questions. How important was the Centre for Policy Studies to Margaret Thatcher? And how important was Margaret Thatcher to the CPS?

Charles Moore: Well, thank you, Robert. I think the CPS was very important to her at a key time. And the key time was early on. She came to the leadership very unexpectedly and very fast. At that moment, there was a tremendous rethinking going on within Conservatism, of which the Centre for Policy Studies had been a key feature. And she had been engaged in that. When Keith Joseph got going with the Centre for Policy Studies, she joined him – she wasn't the key mover, but she was certainly a founder. She was Keith's protege, it would almost be fair to say.

I think it's important to remember how few resources politicians in opposition have. They didn't have the money, they didn't have the staff. They were operating in a shoestring, seat of the pants type of way. And what was needed was a very big rethink. I'm not saying rethinks are better if you have hundreds of people involved – in fact, they're worse. But it's very important to have a few good people to think deeply and boldly. And the CPS was the main instrument of her being able to do that.

RC: One thing that comes out in your first book, though, which may surprise people, is how late both of them come to that sort of hard thinking. With Keith Joseph, he has a historic interest in Friedrich Hayek and Milton Friedman, he's been along to the Institute of Economic Affairs, but once he goes into government under Edward Heath, he does absolutely none of the things that he's talked about. Likewise, with Thatcher, you write that 'until February 1974, her career had been mentally conformist'.

So it feels like it's the failure of the Heath government, which did initially have some reformist instincts, that led her to actually start questioning many of her assumptions. And then Keith Joseph and Alfred Sherman [the CPS's founding Director] are there, with their libraries to plunder, and all the thinkers to introduce her to. It feels almost like it gave her an excuse to go back to university.

CM: Yes. She was always very keen. And that's a good phrase you have, 'going back to university', because though she wasn't in any way academic, she loved to study something. She loved to get into an issue and start thinking about and talking about it. But I don't think Mrs Thatcher fundamentally changed her real beliefs about anything. It was Sherman who said that Mrs Thatcher was a person of beliefs, not ideas, and that beliefs were more important than ideas. So she had those beliefs from childhood, I would say.

RC: Yes, elsewhere in this collection Dominic Sandbrook talks about where Thatcherism comes from – it's her father the shopkeeper, it's the Methodist tendency. There's this through line.

CM: There is. She added some things to that – she was an interesting mixture of liberal economics and conservative attitudes, which is a powerful combination. If you listened to *Any Questions?* or something like that, you could tell that she was broadly from the right of the Conservative Party and had strong beliefs.

But first of all, she was loyal. Remember – she was one of the very few women. She had to prove all the time that she was competent and sensible and not a silly little girl, as they would all tend to think of women at that time. And she didn't want to get out of line.

She was also persuaded – by Keith Joseph, actually – that when Ted Heath stood to be leader in the mid-1960s, he had a passion for getting Britain right. That was the key phrase. Mrs Thatcher never really liked Heath – he was rude to her.

RC: And others…

CM: And others! And very bad with women and so on. But she essentially thought: we've got to beat socialism, we've got to beat Labour. And then they won unexpectedly in 1970, and she became a Cabinet minister. And therefore, she had every interest in advancing the Heath project. Which at the beginning did seem quite a free-market type of enterprise. It was prepared to tackle the trade unions, and there was the famous Selsdon conference…

RC: Yes, when I arrived at the CPS, Selsdon was the WiFi password.

CM: Well, its significance was exaggerated – including by Labour. But it was an attempt to revive free-market ideas in opposition to a *dirigiste* Labour government. And that's where the Heath government started. And of course, it failed. For all sorts of reasons, under pressure of defeat by trade union power, and the oil price shock, and all these things, it turned into a *dirigiste*, corporatist government, with a prices and incomes policy and so on. And Mrs T disliked that. We knew she disliked it at the time, to some extent, and she said so privately. But again, she was not – and she agreed with Keith on this – it was not her place to be the rebel. What licensed her to be the rebel was defeat at the ballot box.

RC: There's a quote in your book when she's talking about the Heath U-turn: 'Those of us who disliked what was happening had not yet either fully analysed the situation or worked out an alternative approach.' And what she's saying there, perhaps with the benefit of hindsight, is that this is what she and Joseph did with the CPS.

CM: I think that's right. There was one person who had worked it out, or at least had worked it out the most. But he was untouchable, because he was such a rebel. And that was Enoch Powell. People always associate him with immigration, but before that he was really a preacher about economic issues.

RC: Yes, there's a Bow Group magazine from the 1960s with a front cover of him as a superhero, with the slogan: 'Enoch vs the Phantom Planners!' Before the 'rivers of blood' speech, he was very much...

CM: ...very much a free-market man and a proto-monetarist and so on, as well as being a high Tory. And Mrs T actually liked him and admired him, although he again was rather patronising and chilly to her. Like Heath, he was pretty bad at dealing with women. But if you were in the Shadow Cabinet or the Cabinet, you couldn't side with Enoch, because he was the rebel over immigration and then over Europe. So he made a brilliant critique of the prices and incomes policy and the U-turn, and she and others agreed with it. But it made it harder to take that view than if he hadn't been around. And then, of course, he told people to vote Labour in both of the 1974 elections, which helped the Tories lose.

So he was now beyond the pale. Powell was a great generator of ideas, but in a funny way, he actually slowed things down.

Anyway, it's 1974, and the Tories are out of office. And Heath makes what from his point of view was the catastrophic mistake of allowing Keith Joseph to set up the Centre for Policy Studies. I think he thought it would improve policy quality and so on, and didn't really understand the ideological implications. But then, off Joseph and Thatcher went.

RC: And this is something I really wanted to get into. Obviously, we at the Centre for Policy Studies love the idea that we reshaped history. There's a line in your book where you say that Heath giving Joseph a free-ranging policy brief was dangerous, but letting him set up the CPS was fatal.

But what was really interesting to me in your biography is how much Thatcher downplays the extent to which she is Joseph's child, especially during the leadership contest. The CPS is doing very interesting and important things. But in the leadership election, and then in the 1979 general election, Thatcher is at pains to claim that this whole word 'Thatcherism' has been invented by Labour, that she's not one of these mad monetarists, and so on. There's a real element of 'don't scare the horses'.

So would Heath really not have fallen in 1975 without the CPS? Or is it that her involvement with the CPS gives her the confidence to set herself up as a challenger, because she knows she will have a different way of doing things?

CM: I think to become leader, she needed to see more clearly than she saw in 1973. Her instincts were right, and were clear. But she had to see how you could do any of this. She had to see how you could do it politically, and how you could do it intellectually and in policy terms.

And of course, her way did not lie clear. Of course rethinks are great, you must have them, but they frighten people. She had to bring along large sections of the Tory party who were suspicious of her and didn't want her. She knew when she became leader that she was in a very small minority at the top of the party. Only an absolute handful of people at the top of the party supported her. So she was the leader of a grassroots rebellion.

RC: Yes, there was a grassroots rebellion. But as you say in the book, above them were the constituency chairmen, who were all traditional buffers who lined up behind Heath.

CM: That's correct. Which in a way was the strength of the Tory party, compared with now. It was a much tighter ship, and had more loyalty and better organisation.

RC: Danny Kruger MP was recently looking back at some of the old minutes from his constituency association. There's a lovely line where they discuss whether they should debate policy issues, and it was concluded that this was not their job.

CM: Well, all that worked very well. In a curious way, the so-called voluntary party was very strong precisely because it wasn't very political. It was a massive social movement, and had a huge buy-in from the middle classes. That's why the Tories had so many members, and why they were quite coherent but not very argumentative. And of course, that all changed due to the pressures of modern times. But Mrs Thatcher had to placate people like that. And to placate Jim Prior. She couldn't really placate Edward Heath, but there was also Willie Whitelaw, Francis Pym, etc. And naturally, the other point to bear in mind when she was actually trying to become leader was that Keith Joseph was already semi-discredited because of his famous Edgbaston speech, which he made just after the second general election that year.

RC: So there's this very interesting dynamic where setting up the CPS gives Joseph the platform to challenge Heath. It gives Margaret Thatcher a platform to realise that she can become the voice of this movement. And then it is a speech for the CPS – where he starts talking about the human stock of the nation and so on – that discredits Joseph as a candidate, and opens the way for Thatcher to become the figurehead. You tell your story in the book, as does one of the other authors in this collection – there's a debate over where exactly it happened, but there is a conversation where she says something like: 'Well, if you won't run, I guess I bloody well have to.'

CM: Yes. And I think the thing about that conversation is that although it happened, she knew already that he wasn't going to stand. So it's not a surprise to her, although she rather presented it as one. He had decided that he couldn't stand, and he was sort of having a conversation about making way for her. And she was by that time ready, once she'd had his imprimatur, to go and stand.

Also, it's very often the case that the person who is considered to be the assassin doesn't get it. Keith wasn't any sort of plotter, but he had been the most important person to attack the Heath legacy…

RC: In the middle of an election campaign!

CM: Yes, he'd spoken at Preston and elsewhere [ahead of the second election in 1974] and said, 'We've got lots of things wrong.' So rather like Heseltine was unlikely to succeed Mrs Thatcher precisely because he'd assassinated her, similarly – though they were very different characters – Keith having sort of assassinated Ted, he couldn't be the next leader. And she sensed that. And that partly explains what you were talking about earlier, because she wanted to be the heir to Keith, an ally of Keith. But she also wanted to say: 'I'm not in a faction, all of you can trust me.'

RC: We'll come back to the chronology, but I'm struck by how – almost even more than Denis – it is a romantic relationship. She talks about Keith, throughout his career, in the fondest of terms. She talks about him as the greatest, the finest, most noble man she ever met. Obviously, he disappoints her as a minister when they're in government. But it does seem to be one of the most extraordinary partnerships.

CM: I mean, partly she laid it on with a trowel because she felt guilty about having to push him out.

RC: Yes, she says later on – very unconvincingly – 'Oh, it should have been Keith.'

CM: She felt an element of guilt for him. And she didn't want to admit what a bad minister he was – which he was in the sense of not being decisive, although he was unbelievably hardworking, intelligent, caring etc. But he was not a natural leader in government.

So yes, she did love Keith – I think in a way that was quite common with her. Though she believed in the superiority of women in a certain sense, she preferred the company of men. And she particularly liked older men and wise men and men who'd seen the world and/or had big thoughts. So she liked generals, and she liked philosophers, and she liked top economists, and entrepreneurs and so on.

She was also very, very alert to which men patronised her as a woman, and to some extent as a lower-class woman. And Keith was always a total gentleman, and advanced her cause from the early days. Though he was a Jew, he was upper class, a baronet, public school. And she immediately knew with people like that whether they were patronising her or not. So for example she didn't like Harold Macmillan, precisely because of that, but she loved Alec Douglas-Home because he was a real gent, in her view. And the same with Keith. And then there was the extra ideological affinity. So this was actually a very typical

Thatcher relationship in a way – she had the same with Reagan, who was also a real gent in her view.

RC: One of the things that emerges from rereading the first of your three books is how contingent all of this was. There are all kinds of points in the early story at which things could have gone another way.

If Heath had given Joseph the job of Shadow Chancellor over Robert Carr – who's completely unknown today – does any of this happen? Then there's this soup of contenders who might pluck up the courage to stand against Heath, which in retrospect looks like the obvious career move. Edward du Cann, Willie Whitelaw – all of them sort of politely back away. And if Joseph hadn't used that phrase about 'human stock', which led to that headline – 'SIR KEITH IN "STOP BABIES" SENSATION'. If he'd run that speech, like all the others, past Margaret Thatcher. If someone else comes into the leadership contest. If Airey Neave doesn't feel slighted and disappointed and puts his shoulder to the wheel as her campaign manager. If Heath actually campaigns properly in his own defence.

No one is expecting Thatcher to win – the Economist describes her as 'precisely the sort of candidate who ought to be able to stand, and lose, harmlessly'. If you play the tape again, it feels like a 1 in 10 chance that you actually end up with a CPS-trained Margaret Thatcher running the Conservative Party.

CM: You're right, of course, and politics is often like that. But there are a couple of qualifications. One is that there wasn't an obvious successor for him. And the other is that she does deserve credit for this thing which she always concealed, but I always try to bring out, since it seems so important. She was a very, very cunning politician. So although her beliefs were absolutely sincere, she was ruthlessly ambitious. And she saw the moment and had the courage to take it when others didn't. And could also see how to woo the people she needed to woo.

And she used, in order to do that, the discontent with Heath, her own economic views, her own more general political prejudices, and also her female attractions. Because remember, she was still in her forties when she became leader. And lots of the backbench Tory MPs who felt very annoyed about Heath, and unrecognised, found her very attractive and charming. It was nothing to do with the politics, really. They'd say: 'She's a brave girl, give her a go', that sort of thing. All these knights of the shires.

RC: But then Reginald Maudling would say, when she becomes leader, 'this is the darkest day in the history of the Tory party'.

CM: But he was very much on the left, and also at the grandest, highest levels of the party. I'm talking more about Sir Somebody Somebody who had sat for Loamshire for 25 years and never been noticed. And they really liked her. They'd often been in the War. And she loved people who'd been in the War. There was a sort of knightly thing about their behaviour, and a damsel in distress bit that she could do. Geoffrey Howe described very well how when she became leader, she was this seemingly frail woman protected, guarded by all these tall men.

RC: And even though Gordon Reece, who's her media Svengali, says he wants no policy at all in the leadership contest, she has already built up this coterie of people via the CPS. There's Alfred Sherman. There was Nigel Vinson, whose historical contribution has I think been significantly underplayed. There's Joseph himself. There is John Hoskyns. There is Hugh Thomas. There is Kingsley Amis. They are collecting this group of people, a movement that forms around her.

CM: Yes, definitely. When this actually happened, I was still at school, just taking my entrance exams to university. So I didn't witness this directly at all, except that Oliver Letwin was a great friend of mine, and his parents were great friends of Keith. And so I would occasionally meet Keith at a dinner with the Letwins. And it was very strong, the sense of all this bubbling up. It wasn't really Tory party stuff. It was more intellectual stuff. But it had a read across, and of course it particularly had a read across to the CPS.

RC: There's a quote from Sherman: 'Early Thatcherism was pure Keith, which meant pure Sherman. She lacked coherence.'

CM: Well, Alfred is right in that sense. What's wrong is that what he calls coherence is in politics a form of madness. Alfred had very much a Communist mind, though he had abandoned Communism. A sort of programmatic mind about how everything should be, and there's only one right answer. Which is basically a bad way of thinking about the world.

But he had great brilliance and perception and courage and determination, which is so often lacking in British politicians. And so he could push through these ideas, often terribly damaging as expressed by Alfred. But if filtered and rendered usable by actual practical politicians, extremely valuable.

RC: You have the stories of her Shadow Cabinet once she's elected leader getting very upset because they're hanging around for hours waiting to see her, because she's closeted with Sherman. And when they do go in, she's like: 'But Alfred says…'

CM: Well, there was that. But Alfred didn't make it easy for himself. He had this extremely rebarbative personality, and was often shatteringly rude to people. He always had that thing of the intellectual who's trying to do things in politics of being status conscious.

RC: Someone once told me that Keith Joseph's most valuable contribution to the CPS was providing a buffer zone between Alfred Sherman and Margaret Thatcher.

CM: Yes, I think that's right. I knew Alfred a bit later on, because I joined the Telegraph in 1979. And he was a part-time leader writer. And again, it was the same – this violently fierce style of argument, and an acute consciousness of his own rights and privileges. A very prickly person. But with this piercing mind that would see things that more conventional people wouldn't see.

And he really was extremely helpful to her and Keith, and the CPS through him. Inevitably, of course, they fell out after a bit of time in office. It was probably inevitable in that kind of role, as with Dominic Cummings, but it was also very much to do with Alfred's particular personality. And also, he was trying to sort of weaponise and sometimes commercialise his access. This was later on. So you can understand why the officials would try to keep him out of the room. And it all became too difficult for Mrs Thatcher. So in the end, she let him go, as they nowadays say.

RC: On this point about philosophy, you mentioned Oliver Letwin – there's actually a very interesting psychodrama there. In his auto-biography, he essentially blames his mother Shirley for putting the Conservative Party on the wrong course because it's her who tells Keith Joseph, around the time the CPS is potentially going to be called the Social Market Foundation, that you need to stop talking about all this 'social market' stuff, and just focus on economics and individuals. In doing so, in Oliver's account, they lost touch with community and family and society, and those aspects were only triumphantly fused back into the Conservative narrative when Oliver Letwin and David Cameron took over the party some decades later.

CM: Yes, I think the flaw in Oliver's analysis is that politicians must address the most urgent problem of the age. And the most urgent domestic problems in this time were economic – which also had a social aspect, because inflation has terrible social effects, as do excessive trade union power and strikes. By the same token, I think Oliver was right later on. His remedies perhaps weren't very successful, but he was right to push towards a greater concentration on social issues when he was helping David Cameron, the Big Society and so on, because those were more the problems of that age.

RC: But it must have been extraordinary, being there at that time. David Willetts talks in his essay about being in the Oxford Union to hear Keith Joseph speak. It must have been like being a music fan in 1964 or 1965, when the Beatles and others burst onto the scene. There's suddenly this sense that there is something happening.

CM: That's a good way to put it. I was brought up a Liberal with a big L. And when I went to Cambridge, I joined the party. In fact I think I'm technically still in it, because my father paid for a life membership. And I wasn't actually at all political at that time. I mean, I was interested in political thought and so on. But I wasn't engaged in political activity or anything like that, just endless discussions and argument. And I do definitely remember that the Thatcher–Joseph impact was exciting.

It didn't make me a Tory at that stage. I didn't vote Conservative in my first vote – I should say my second vote, because my first vote was to stay in the European Community. I voted Liberal in 1979. But I remember being very pleased that Mrs Thatcher had won. And she was definitely the only one – with Keith – who was saying things which seemed to be interesting, and which made you think.

It's very hard to exaggerate how dead intellectually Labour was at that stage. Except, in a way, for the far left. The Tory wets, as they later became called, were also intellectually weak. You very much felt – rather like you do now – that nobody was getting anything right, and nothing was happening. I mean, I didn't mind it as an undergraduate, because I was having fun. But I could see the state of the country, the fact that there seemed to be no answer to any difficult problem. And so when you heard these very clear things coming through, your ears did prick up.

RC: That's actually brought us back to where I wanted to get to. You said that the CPS was most influential in the early years, and I think that's absolutely right. But when Thatcher becomes leader, Nigel Vinson – who is one of the four or five people who were present at the creation of the CPS, and remains part of the original core, and in fact bankrolls the whole thing – asks whether there is even a need for the CPS 'now the Tory Party is in the hands of true believers'.

But of course, it wasn't in their hands. In fact there is a case that actually the CPS is most influential, and necessary, after she becomes leader rather than before. Because the Tory wets do not see themselves as intellectually moribund. They are the majority, and they are determined to resist these dangerous, newfangled ideas which are percolating into the party. So you have this three-year civil war, in which for example Keith Joseph and Jim Prior are ordered to work together, which is a bit like ordering Jeremy Corbyn and Kemi Badenoch to come together and agree on a programme.

CM: Yes, I think the CPS was very important in those years when she's leader but she hasn't yet become Prime Minister – but in a different way.

We've discussed how important it was at first, in terms of really making her concentrate on key issues. This basic diagnosis about union power, inflation, economic management, monetarism, the size of the state, it's setting the framework for what becomes her mission, absolutely.

And then 1975–9 is more an internal battle, in which the CPS was very important. Not a battle to get control of her mind, because I think her mind was fairly clear. But to help her prevail against a Tory party establishment which was essentially against her.

A very important person in this, in fact probably even more important than Keith, in terms of the overall balance of the party, was Geoffrey Howe. Howe is in many ways on the left of the Conservative Party, but he was on the right – for want of a better word – on all the economic questions. She and Geoffrey were never terribly close, and she was always sensitive because he had been a candidate in the first ballot of the leadership election against Heath, to her surprise and disappointment.

RC: Because she'd always thought he was on her side.

CM: Yes, yes. There was always that element. And she got irritated by him as well.

RC: With fateful consequences…

CM: Of course! It all accumulated over time. But Geoffrey was very good on these economic questions. He had thought about them as much as Keith. And he'd been very close to the Institute of Economic Affairs for a very long time, which was the other important think tank – much more theoretical than the CPS, but a very important, long-term evangelist for free markets.

And so, in those years, you had Geoffrey and you had people like John Hoskyns – who is the co-author of the 'Stepping Stones' report, and becomes the first head of her Policy Unit – and you had the others at the CPS. He was a very, very nice man, John, but also very tough in his arguments. He would get very annoyed with everybody else, and often annoyed with her.

RC: Yes, he ends up sending her probably the rudest memo ever addressed by an underling to a prime minister, effectively saying you're being completely useless.

CM: Yes, she was amazingly tolerant of that sort of thing. But during those opposition years, you see these battles over policy documents, like 'The Right Approach' and 'The Right Approach to the Economy'. And remember: the wets were running the machine. Ian Gilmour to some extent, and Chris Patten in the Conservative Research Department. So there's a big battle going on there all the time.

RC: Which is why you have this weird thing in 1979 where Jim Prior is controlling the election manifesto and Thatcher is sending back draft after draft saying: 'This is rubbish. This isn't tough enough.'

CM: And that was all very difficult. But it was also quite valuable, because it did hammer out such compromises as were necessary. And it did also over time expose the fact that the wets were more incoherent than she was.

RC: But of course, if you're an Alfred Sherman or a John Hoskyns, you're feeling deeply frustrated. You're feeling you're trapped in moderation: we have taken over the party and yet we are not going full blast. There are actually echoes of today's debate: shouldn't we just be properly sound and properly Conservative, rather than making these endless compromises?

CM: Mrs Thatcher was very good at that. She was a great preacher, and could go on and on – to the point of boredom – about her particular beliefs. But she was very conscious that things had to actually be achieved, whereas it's a natural instinct of the intellectual just to keep talking.

This was very important in seeing the whole thing through: she was prepared to take a huge amount of punishment. Not just to reiterate that she was right, though she did reiterate that a lot. But actually to try to make things happen. Whereas intellectuals just tend to sound off. And of course, lots of things did go wrong in office in the early days. First of all because the interest rate policy was probably too brutal.

RC: Yes, there's this desperate moment where the CPS faction, people like Hoskyns, have to sort of smuggle Jürg Niehans into Downing Street – the economist Patten writes off as a 'crazy Swiss professor' – to explain to her that she's got monetarism wrong, and that they need to loosen policy.

CM: She was trying very hard – and I think broadly successfully – to implement these economic beliefs. But there were lots of setbacks. And of course, there were U-turns. In 1981 she gives in to the miners, because she wasn't ready. And on industrial policy, which Keith Joseph is running, there are lots of U-turns and subsidies there. Which caused Alfred Sherman to turn Keith's portrait to the wall in the CPS offices.

RC: This is when they bail out British Leyland. And they also bail out ICL, which in the long run becomes Fujitsu, because they've been told that otherwise all of the computers in government will switch off.

But this is one of the interesting tensions in this story. One of the arguments historians now tend to make, especially historians on the left, is essentially that Thatcher has been overdramatised. That all of the things she did, or at least most of them, would have happened anyway.

But if you read your biography, it does drive home how – again, how contingent Margaret Thatcher was, how unusual she was. Has any other serving Tory leader gone to meetings of the Conservative Philosophy Group? Has any Labour leader gone to the left-wing equivalent, apart from maybe Jeremy Corbyn? Has anyone read Hayek, or Friedman, or slammed them down on people's desks and said 'this is what we believe'?

You'll know this too, but 99% of ministers you meet will say things like: 'I'm as free market as anyone, but…' It is so unusual to find someone who, even though she has to make tactical compromises, has this kind of guiding vision.

CM: Yes, I think it was quite a religious approach. I mean, she was personally religious. But it's a characteristic of religious belief that through thick and thin, you hold your belief, and you have a guiding star. It doesn't mean you have a consistent pattern of action, necessarily. But you have an almost cosmic view of what it is you're trying to do. And that is very different from most politicians.

And in an odd way, that didn't make her very ideological. She wasn't ideologically rigid. It would be a mistake to think that. But she wanted to do the things she believed in, and this emanated outwards. And that's why I think the argument that it would have happened anyway is wrong. Because what's so unusual about her form of government is that she imposed what Ferdinand Mount, who ran her Policy Unit after Hoskyns, described as 'the angry will' on the whole of Whitehall.

So as the years passed, gradually, everybody in Whitehall and Westminster knew what she wanted. She wasn't actually going to get everything she wanted. Sometimes she was getting things she definitely didn't want. But they knew what she wanted. And the CPS helped refine that. And this is a very, very powerful thing in politics, and a very rare thing. I mean, we don't really know what Rishi Sunak wants, do we, or Theresa May, or in many respects, Boris Johnson.

RC: I mean, even in this memo that Hoskyns writes, called 'Your Political Survival'. Even though he sets out all manner of ways in which he thinks she's getting it wrong, he does say: 'There is no other politician who is likely even to attempt to lead the country in the right direction.'

CM: That's right. Because without her, as often happened to the Conservatives, they would have succumbed to cultural pessimism. 'Oh, that will be nice, but it can't be done.'

RC: But even Hoskyns, as he leaves he says it's because she's never going to take on the Civil Service. And unless we do that, we can never accomplish anything. Which a lot of people would say today…

CM: Yes, and they're both right and wrong. You never will accomplish all the things you wish to accomplish. But it's remarkable what you can accomplish if you're very determined to do it. And you have to make some sacrifices along the way and jettison some things and so on. And she was wily enough about that, and determined enough about that, to keep winning elections.

And this is the other thing. Except for Tony Blair, she's the only one in modern times who actually had the time in office, with decent majorities, to do something. And this is partly to do with the focus that the CPS and Keith Joseph gave her early on.

RC: Moving through the years slightly, you can tell the story through your books. In the index of the first one, there are a huge number of mentions of the CPS, or Keith Joseph, or Alfred Sherman. In the second book, they start to go away. And in the third book, they come back, but usually because she's speaking at their memorial services. It's in the titles, too: the second one is *Everything She Wants*, and she has the whole Civil Service to deliver that for her. And then, of course, the trilogy concludes with *Herself Alone*.

So there's this sense of progression. In the first period, she needs allies. And then partly after the Falklands, and especially after the 1983 election, there is this shift where suddenly you can see the people in Downing Street thinking, to paraphrase Tony Blair, that they can reorder the world around them. There's been an incredible nervousness and worry around this project, right up to the 1979 election and through the early years. And then it transitions into this almost sort of imperial mood, where they suddenly start thinking about privatisation and all these other ideas.

CM: Yes, there definitely was that shift. But one of the reasons why she didn't lose her ideological grip, if ideological is the right word, is that the role of the Centre for Policy Studies in opposition was increasingly taken by the No 10 Policy Unit in power. And the people who staffed it were a pretty able group, many of whom had CPS or to a lesser extent IEA links. John Redwood, David Willetts, Oliver Letwin, etc. They knew how she thought, and they were pretty expert on policy as well. And they were supplemented by or partnered with civil servants who were less ideological, but were up for the challenge. And that was a pretty powerful thing. And in that middle period it worked very well.

RC: And this is one of the fascinating things, looking back at the CPS's history. It's still playing a vital role, but it's a completely different one. At the start, as you say, it is this guerrilla unit, this gang of outriders. But when Hugh Thomas is appointed Chairman, he and Alfred Sherman have this showdown where Thomas says: 'Our job is to get on with all sections of the Tory party, and serve the Tory party.' And Sherman says: 'Absolutely not. We need to carry on the crusade.' And he loses.

So once she is fully in command, you have this system – which is definitely something which evolves rather than being designed – in which people will intern for the CPS, or write pamphlets for the CPS, or be talent-spotted by Nigel Lawson, or what have you. And then they will go into the Policy Unit and try to put these ideas into practice. And as soon as they leave No 10, they will start writing pamphlets for the CPS again. So John Redwood, David Willetts, Brian Griffiths, Oliver Letwin, they're all writing about privatisation, or reforming the NHS, or the pension system, or education, or whatever they couldn't get through when they were in government, or didn't get around to. And that feeds into what their successors and allies are doing in No 10 and the departments. So you're simultaneously testing the waters but also pushing at the frontiers.

CM: Yes. And it wasn't too strictly drawn. So for example Ferdy Mount was important when he ran the Policy Unit...

RC: He hated Alfred Sherman, I think?

CM: Yes. And not really a Thatcherite. But an intellectual who was genuinely interested in policy, and I think did a lot for the CPS.

RC: Brian Griffiths, now Lord Griffiths, runs the Policy Unit and later chairs the CPS. And David Willetts goes from running the No 10 Policy Unit to running the CPS and the Conservative Research Department simultaneously. He has senior roles at both. So he would just take his party hat off and put his think tank hat on.

CM: The other thing to mention is that you talked about Hugh Thomas and Alfred. But another faultline opened up a bit after that, which is Europe. I can remember the CPS having great difficulties about that. With Hugh and Oliver Knox, who ran the publication programme, being very pro-European, and a lot of other people being highly Eurosceptic. There were a lot of battles about that at the end of the decade.

RC: And that's actually another way in which the story of the CPS is the story of the Thatcher era, and of the Conservative movement. So you have the insurgent phase, you have the establishment phase, and then you have the phase where you can see the future arguments coming.

I mean, again, bizarre as it will seem to anyone who lived through the Brexit wars, there is a point at which Oliver Letwin is the most Eurosceptic person in the Conservative Party. And by his own account, he writes a pamphlet for the CPS – I think it actually comes out after Thatcher's famous Bruges speech, but he's thinking about it and writing it beforehand. And his pamphlet says Europe is becoming a superstate.

CM: Yes.

RC: And this is heresy. I mean, Hugh Thomas says: 'This is not Thatcherism. This is not what we believe.' And you can see that faultline starting to open, and it's happening within the Cabinet over the Exchange Rate Mechanism, and the Jacques Delors speech to the TUC.

CM: Yes, that's right. Although while the Bruges speech was clearly welcomed by Eurosceptics, it wasn't an anti-European speech. It was an anti-Delors speech. It was an anti-'Little Europe' speech. All the stuff about Warsaw, Budapest and Prague also being European cities was an attempt to get rid of the superstate idea, get rid of the single currency idea, and have a much bigger, wider free Europe.

RC: And there was the Single Market, which was in many ways a Thatcherite project.

CM: It was, though she used to say afterwards that she had underrated the extent to which it was a political project. They kept selling it using the word 'market', the people who wanted her to buy it, and glossing over the constitutional aspects of it.

RC: By this point, there has been this fracturing of the right, and then her fall, which is obviously a moment of trauma. How long does it take the Conservative Party to recover from it? Does it ever recover?

CM: Well, I thought that it had recovered to a large extent in the early Cameron era. And these antipathies had greatly declined over the years. But of course it all recrudesced because of the referendum. It's been extremely bad since then. And lots of other things have been added on top of that, and now everybody hates everybody else. And that won't be resolved until after defeat, which I suppose is likely, and then there'll be some titanic battle.

But in terms of the fall of Thatcher – I think it was reasonable that she should go by then. She had probably outstayed her welcome. But the way it was done was catastrophic for the way people thought about one another within the Conservative tribe.

RC: And also for the Centre for Policy Studies. Obviously, Keith Joseph is the presiding spirit. But on the wall of my office there is a portrait of Margaret Thatcher, literally sitting over my shoulder. It is hard for anyone not to feel inadequate, in the shadow of that legacy.

CM: Of course. And it must be difficult for the CPS, because it's your proudest thing. But you have to be new in every generation.

RC: Well, that's a question. Is the relationship between Joseph and Thatcher and the CPS, and that moment in time – the way it carries and propels her and supports her and helps to entrench her – is that just a sort of beautiful, freak moment in history? Or is it a model that could crop up again?

CM: Well, I don't know if it's a model, but I don't think it's a freak moment in history either. Because I think cometh the hour, cometh the man – or in this case, the woman. And when things are very difficult, something interesting happens. And this is what we're waiting for now, isn't it?

I'm not a great believer in *Führerprinzip*. But in a way, in a very strange way, it happened with Boris and winning the referendum. Despite Boris' manifold faults, that was completely remarkable. And then to win the general election, that was a most remarkable coup, and that really was down to him. And maybe he would have had longer-lasting success had Covid not come along, or maybe not, because Boris is just too wayward.

But anyway, I think we are now in a very difficult time for the whole of the Western world. And Mrs Thatcher was also facing a very difficult time for the whole of the Western world – we mustn't forget that it was not just Britain. And this was true not only of economic matters, but of the Cold War.

And now with Russia and China and a prolonged financial crisis and Iran and the Middle East and wokery – there are a great many serious and related issues, which we are confronting very poorly. And I think we do need to think hard about how we are led, therefore. And we haven't worked out how to do that yet.

People are very much trapped. It takes a long time to get out of the moving spirit of an age and recognise when the new age has come. And she did recognise that. So we shouldn't be nostalgic about Thatcher. We should notice how she looked forward. She recognised the end of that collectivist age in the 1970s and wanted to bring it about.

And similarly, today the age that is still haunting us is the age when we kept pretending everything was going to be alright. Things can only get better, yesterday's gone, the end of history, etc, etc. Which is still the model for our consumerist economics – too much borrowing, the peace dividend, all that sort of thing. And Mrs Thatcher, though an optimistic person, always had a very, very strong sense of threat. That democracies are fragile. The world is fragile.

RC: A sense that Britain was in danger.

CM: Yes. Not just culturally and politically, but in the sense of being threatened by hostile powers. And I don't think it was paranoid. I think it was true. And it's true now that we have an axis of definite enemies in a way that even in the Cold War we didn't have, because China and Russia were such incredible enemies themselves. We were able to play them off against one another. But now you've got that and militant Islam, you've got a pretty noxious cauldron of international threat. And Britain is just one potential victim of that. It's not a unique British problem at all.

RC: On top of which there are all the issues of economic dynamism that the CPS was founded to address in the first place, that sense of a need to revive the spirit of enterprise.

CM: Yes. We read every day about how bad our productivity is, but with very little sign of anything being done about it. We don't have trade union power to the same extent. But it is coming back. And what we've got, which is a sort of substitute for trade union power, is permanent officialdom, spreading control through the system and taking away political authority from elected politicians. And we've also got it in the workplace, so that what would have been shop stewards, ruining businesses and corrupting enterprises, are now HR departments. And enforcing compliance and diversity rules and all that sort of thing. So suddenly – not suddenly, actually, but slowly – all these same tentacles have crept up again. A different form, but the same problem.

RC: So plenty for us to work on over the next 50 years.

CM: I'd say so.

RC: Charles Moore, thank you very much.

Charles Moore (Lord Moore of Etchingham) is a former Editor of the Spectator, Sunday Telegraph and Daily Telegraph. His authorised biography of Margaret Thatcher was published in three volumes between 2013 and 2019.

2 Liberty and Limited Government

....

MARGARET THATCHER

This essay was originally delivered as the inaugural Keith Joseph Memorial Lecture in 1996.

Keith Joseph, in whose honour this Lecture is delivered, had the charm of a hundred paradoxes.

He was a modest man; but, unlike so many modest men, he had really nothing to be modest about.

He was (that overworked, but in this case appropriate word) 'brilliant'; yet he never indulged in intellectual virtuosity.

He was brave; yet by nature he was timid.

He could seem cerebral and remote; but he had a warm heart and impish humour that made his friendship an inexpressible delight.

Keith was also unusual in that, even when quite old and frail, he seemed somehow to remain young. The secret of this youthful spirit was the opposite to that of Faust. For in Keith's case it was the fruit of innocence.

Not the innocence of inexperience, let alone of insensitivity. This was the innocence of the pure of heart – of those who have wrestled with the evils of humanity, while remaining unspotted by the world.

Keith's goodness was shown by the little kindnesses which marked his dealings with both political friends and opponents – he had no enemies.

But Keith was more than good; he was also great. And his greatness lay in his integrity.

Integrity is an old-fashioned word. There are even some who will tell you it is an old-fashioned thing. But, for a politician, integrity is everything.

It is not just a matter of avoiding bribes and inducements. In our remarkably financially honest British politics, it is not even mainly about that – whatever learned judges may say about the matter.

In politics, integrity really lies in the conviction that it's only on the basis of truth that power should be won – or indeed can be worth winning. It lies in an unswerving belief that you have to be right.

It was not that Keith wore a hair shirt from preference. He was averse to any kind of suffering, especially other people's – and applying the right remedies to the British disease was bound to require suffering.

But Keith's integrity was absolute.

When he became convinced – finally convinced, after the endless discussions which were a mark of his open-minded, open-hearted style – that a proposition was correct, he felt he had to defend it. He had to fight for it. When he faced those raging, spitting Trotskyist crowds at our great liberal centres of learning, I suspect he wondered sometimes whether he would have to die for it. But there he stood. He could do no other.

This Lecture is not, however, intended as a eulogy. The purpose of recalling the turbulent times of 20 years ago when Keith Joseph and I reshaped Conservatism – with the help of a handful of others, whose dedication compensated for their fewness – is that the same qualities as Keith's are required in our party today.

Rethinking Conservative policy
Keith Joseph's name will always be closely associated with the rethinking of Conservative principles and policies in preparation for the Conservative government of the 1980s.

You will recall that the party was out of office – having lost the February 1974 election – when Keith began delivering, in the summer and autumn, a series of speeches analysing what had gone wrong, and suggesting a change of direction.

In June came the Upminster speech. Keith dared to talk about what he called the 'inherent contradictions [of the]… mixed economy'.

This, in the eyes of the Tory establishment, whose only real criticism of the socialists was that they were mixing the economy in the wrong proportions, was bad enough.

But it was the Preston speech in September – delivered almost on the eve of a second general election – which most horrified Keith's critics. In it, he dared to tell the truth about inflation: and that truth was inevitably damning for the previous Conservative government, of which he and I had been a part.

Inflation was properly to be ascribed to the excessive growth of the money supply. And since, as Keith devastatingly observed, there was a time lag of as much as a year or two between the monetary cause and the inflationary effect, the high inflation of the summer of 1974 – 17% and rising – was the responsibility of the Conservatives.

Keith also rightly noted that the root of the Conservative government's failure to control inflation was fear of unemployment. But – as he and I would go on to argue on other occasions – unemployment was not an alternative to inflation, but one result of it.

Ever higher doses of inflation were required in order to have even a short-term effect on jobs. And in the longer term inflation undermined confidence, pushed up wage costs, promoted inefficiency and aborted new employment.

For saying such things, Keith was publicly ridiculed and privately vilified. His colleagues accused him of disloyalty, splitting the party and so on.

Those whom Hayek had described as 'the socialists of all parties' united to denounce him. For Keith in their eyes was demonstrating the worst possible political seamanship. He was 'rocking the boat'. But in fact it was Keith's compass that was true – and it was the boat that was already adrift and threatened by total shipwreck.

Most of the economic analysis which Keith Joseph offered has since been accepted. But Keith was not only, or even primarily, interested in economics. It was simply that in the 1970s the economics had gone so devastatingly wrong that this was where any new analysis had to focus. Indeed, that remained true to a large extent in the 1980s.

Reversing Britain's economic decline was such a huge and painful undertaking that, at least until the later years, the economy had to come first.

Keith himself, though, was even more interested in social than in economic issues. He had come into politics not from personal ambition but from an idealistic urge to diminish the misery of poverty. But his one foray at this time into rethinking social policy, in the form of the Edgbaston speech, went badly wrong.

In fact, though flawed in some respects, the speech – with its emphasis on remoralising society and on strengthening the family – deserves rereading.

It does not, though, reveal much about his essential philosophy, which with Keith – as with most professional politicians – remained below the surface.

The kind of conservatism which he and I – though coming from very different backgrounds – favoured would be best described as 'liberal', in the old-fashioned sense. And I mean the liberalism of Mr Gladstone, not of the latter-day collectivists.

That is to say, we placed far greater confidence in individuals, families, businesses and neighbourhoods than in the state.

But the view which became an orthodoxy in the early part of this century – and a dogma by the middle of it – was that the story of human progress in the modern world was the story of increasing state power.

Progressive legislation and political movements were assumed to be the ones which extended the intervention of government.

It was in revolt against this trend and the policies it bred that Hayek wrote *The Road to Serfdom*, which had such a great effect upon me when I first read it – and a greater effect still, when Keith suggested that I go deeper into Hayek's other writings.

Hayek wrote:

'How sharp a break – with the whole evolution of Western civilisation the modern trend towards socialism means – becomes clear if we consider it not merely against the background of the 19th century, but in a longer historical perspective. We are rapidly abandoning not the views merely of Cobden and Bright, of Adam Smith and Hume, or even of Locke and Milton, but one of the salient characteristics of Western civilisation as it has grown from the foundations laid by Christianity and the Greeks and Romans. Not merely 19th- and 18th-century liberalism, but the basic individualism inherited by us from Erasmus and Montaigne, from Cicero and Tacitus, Pericles and Thucydides is progressively relinquished.'

So, ladies and gentlemen, against that background, it is not surprising that the left claimed all the arguments of principle, and that all that remained to the right were the arguments of accountancy – essentially, when and how socialism could be afforded.

It was this fundamental weakness at the heart of Conservatism which ensured that even Conservative politicians regarded themselves as destined merely to manage a steady shift to some kind of socialist state. This was what – under Keith's tuition – we came to call the 'ratchet effect'.

But all that was not just bad politics. It was false philosophy – and counterfeit history.

Let me remind you why this is so.

Creativity is necessarily a quality which pertains to individuals. Indeed, perhaps the one immutable law of anthropology is that we are all different. Now, of course, individuals can't fulfil their potential without a society in which to do so.

And to set the record straight – once again – I have never minimised the importance of society, only contested the assumption that society means the state rather than other people.

Conservatives do not take an extreme atomistic view of society.

We need no lectures now, or at any other time, about the importance of custom, convention, tradition, belief, national institutions or what the ancient Romans would describe as 'piety'.

Nor do we dispute that the bonds of society need ultimately to be guaranteed by the state.

It is Marxists, not Conservatives, who imagined – or at least pretended to imagine – that the state would wither away.

No. What marks out our Conservative vision is the insight that the state – government – only underpins the conditions for a prosperous and fulfilling life. It does not generate them.

Moreover, the very existence of this state, with its huge capacity for evil, is a potential threat to all the moral, cultural, social and economic benefits of freedom.

States, societies and economies, which allow the distinctive talents of individuals to flourish, themselves also flourish. Those which dwarf, crush, distort, manipulate or ignore them cannot progress.

Those eras in which a high value has been placed on the individual are the ones which have known the greatest advances.

By contrast, although the great monolithic states, empires and systems can produce impressive monuments and a high level of cultural sophistication, they are not able to mobilise the initiative of their populations to ensure that each generation can expect a better life than its predecessor.

It is only Western civilisation that has discovered the secret of continual progress. This is because only Western civilisation has developed a culture in which individuals matter, a society in which private property is secure, and a political system in which a range of competing views and interests are accommodated.

The moral foundation of this system – which is so spontaneous as hardly to seem a system – is the Judaeo-Christian outlook.

The system's institutional foundation is the rule of law.

Expressed like this, it all sounds very abstract. But we in Britain are extraordinarily, indeed uniquely, lucky. Because, with us, these things have become second nature and a way of life.

Over the centuries, the habits of freedom became ever more established in these islands. They and the institutions which came to embody them – independent courts, the common law, above all Parliament – were in a special sense democratised: that is, they came to be regarded as the birthright not of any class or group, but of the nation as a whole. In a more doctrinal form they have found their way into the Constitution of the United States.

All this meant that when Keith and I were struggling to shift Britain back from the socialist state, we were also acting as conservatives, with a small 'c'.

We were seeking to re-establish an understanding of the fundamental truths which had made Western life, British life, and the life of the English-speaking peoples what they were.

This was the foundation of our Conservative revolution. It remains the foundation for any successful Conservative programme of government.

And that is the first lesson which needs to be drawn from the rethinking of Conservatism, which Keith inspired and led. The principles which he restated, and which formed the basis of the policies the Conservative government pursued while I was Prime Minister, are as true and as relevant now as they were two decades ago – or indeed, give or take a little economics, two centuries ago.

The cause of limited government – in which the state is servant not master, custodian not collaborator, umpire not player – is the one beneath whose standard Keith Joseph and I gathered all those years ago.

It is time to take it out of mothballs, brush off the odd collectivist cobweb that's hung on to it, and go forth to meet the foe.

The second lesson is that avoiding debate about the large issues of government and politics leads to directionless failure. Being prepared to state uncomfortable truths, as Keith insisted on doing, is the precondition for success.

It is extremely doubtful whether the Conservative Party lost support because of Keith's controversial Preston speech in September 1974. But I am quite sure that without it we would never have embraced the approach that yielded, first victory in 1979, and then a remarkable string of achievements in the years which followed.

Splits and disagreements over important issues never did a party so much harm as the absence of honest, principled debate.

There is, however, one apparent lesson that we would be most unwise to draw. That is the suggestion, which one hears from time to time, that the only hope for the Conservative Party is a period in opposition.

The situation today in the party is entirely different from that in 1974, when Keith was making his great speeches. In the present Prime Minister, the party has a leader who shares the broad analysis that Keith Joseph and I put forward.

It is no secret that between John Major and me there have been differences... on occasion.

But these have always been differences about how to achieve objectives, rather than what those objectives should be.

What is required now is to ensure that those objectives are clearly explained, so that a re-elected Conservative government can go further towards fulfilling them.

The attractions of opposition are greatly exaggerated by those who have not experienced it.

What has gone wrong?

But, judging from the opinion polls, opposition is where the electorate is at present inclined to send us. For a variety of reasons, which I shall describe shortly, I believe that this would be ill-judged on their part.

The Conservative Party still has much to offer.

And from Mr Blair's New – or not so new – Labour Party there is much to fear.

But we must not ignore the present discontent.

Some of it is more or less inevitable. A constant struggle is required to ensure that long-serving governments don't run out of steam. I always regarded it as necessary to combine my role as Prime Minister with that of Chief Stoker so as to keep up the pressure.

It is also true that the political world is more complicated than in the 1980s. The sharp divide between the forces of freedom represented by the Conservative Party and the West on the one hand, and the forces of collectivism represented by the Labour Party and the Soviet bloc on the other, is a thing of the past.

The extent of the success we achieved in the 1980s has, in this sense, caught up with us.

That may be politically inconvenient; but I for one would not change it.

During most of my political life, freedom in this country was under a direct challenge from fellow-travelling socialists and an aggressive Soviet Union.

These challenges were overcome because the Conservative Party in Britain and other right-of-centre parties elsewhere – under the international leadership of Ronald Reagan – proved too much for them.

The fashionable expression is that Communism and indeed social-ism 'imploded'. If that means that their system was always unviable, so be it – though many of the people who now say this scarcely seemed to believe it true before the 'implosion' occurred.

But, anyway, let's not forget that the system collapsed because it was squeezed by the pressure that we on the right – I repeat, on the right – of politics applied.

And the left should not be allowed to get away with pretending otherwise.

But, of course, in politics there is only gratitude for benefits yet to be received. That is why, however successful they've proved to be, governments and parties have to keep on re-applying their enduring principles to new circumstances.

The Conservative Party today has problems not because our analysis has been wrong or our principles faulty.

Our difficulties are due to the fact that, in certain limited but important respects, our policies and performance have not lived up to our analysis and principles.

That is why the current idea, put around by some malcontents, that the Conservative Party is in trouble because it has moved to the right, and that this is what needs to be remedied, is baloney – and Denis might be able to suggest a still more telling description.

The test is simple. Just ask yourself: is it because the Government has not spent, borrowed and taxed enough that people are discontented?

Or is it that we have gone too far towards increasing government spending, borrowing and taxation?

The answer is obvious. We are unpopular, above all, because the middle classes – and all those who aspire to join the middle classes – feel that they no longer have the incentives and opportunities they expect from a Conservative government.

I am not sure what is meant by those who say that the party should return to something called 'One Nation Conservatism'.

As far as I can tell by their views on European federalism, such people's creed would be better described as 'No Nation Conservatism'.

And certainly anyone who believes that salvation is to be found further away from the basic Conservative principles which prevailed in the 1980s – small government, a property-owning democracy, tax cuts, deregulation and national sovereignty – is profoundly mistaken.

That mistake in most cases has its origins in the acceptance of the picture of the 1980s which has been painted by the critics. That decade changed the direction of Britain to such an extent that it is unlikely that even a Labour government would altogether reverse it – try as they might.

Inflation was brought down, without the use of the prices and incomes controls which the great and the good all agreed were indispensable.

Public spending as a share of GDP fell, which allowed tax rates to be cut – and government borrowing was reduced. We repaid debt. 364 economists who claimed that it was madness to think you could get economic growth by cutting government borrowing were proved wrong: I'm told they were never the same again.

Reform of the public finances was matched by reform of the trade unions, deregulation and privatisation of industries and a great extension of ownership of houses, shares and savings – quite a lot of 'stakeholding' in fact!

The economic growth and the improvement of living standards which resulted from these reforms were so great that for a time materialism, rather than poverty, became the main accusation against us. 'Hunting the yuppie' became the favourite sport of the neo-puritan, liverish left.

But, of course, the reality was that the success which free enterprise brought over those years was not just expressed in conspicuous consumption – though what would we give for a few more of those yuppies today!

It also allowed a doubling – that's over and above inflation – of voluntary giving to good causes.

Moreover, though we made mistakes of financial management by allowing the economy to overheat and inflation to rise towards the end of that period, the general advance of prosperity was solidly based upon real economic improvements.

Above all, there was a rapid and sustained rise in industrial productivity, which has continued. And as a result of the control of public expenditure over those years – particularly the reining back of future commitments on pensions – Britain advances towards the next millennium with a large advantage over our European competitors as regards taxation and costs.

The message from all this is not that everything in the 1980s was perfect or that everything that has followed it in the 1990s has been bad.

Every prime minister has his – and her – regrets.

The important message, rather, is that in Britain we have seen from the 1980s what works – just as we saw in the 1970s what did not.

And what works here, as elsewhere, is free enterprise and not big government.

So it would make no economic sense at all for us to move closer to the policies of our opponents.

Rather, the economic challenge is to cut back the burden of state spending, borrowing and taxation still further.

And trying to move towards the centre ground makes no political sense either.

As Keith used to remind us, it is not the centre ground but the common ground – the shared instincts and traditions of the British people – on which we should pitch our tents. That ground is solid – whereas the centre ground is as slippery as the spin doctors who have colonised it.

The Labour Party

Ladies and Gentlemen, one of Keith Joseph's most admirable characteristics – and one which secured for him respect and affection – was that he never cast doubt on the motives of his opponent. So, following in his footsteps, I am not going to cast doubt on the motives of the Leader of the Opposition.

But what about the party he leads? The Labour Party itself may have changed many of its policies, but it hasn't changed its spots. You can tell this from the unpleasant noises it makes when anything like profits are mentioned.

There is still virtually nothing that Labour spokesmen wouldn't spend more taxpayers' money on, or wish to control more tightly. They have learned to accompany these prescriptions with Conservative-sounding rhetoric, and even some Conservative-sounding policies.

But the distinctive mark of every Labour policy, from health to education, from privatised utilities to the labour market, is more government interference.

All sorts of worthy people believe that Mr Blair in office would control his party, and not they him. But this would be a large gamble to take.

Moreover, Mr Blair is not only human; he is also (as his record shows) by instinct a man of the left.

Confronted with the sort of choices you face in government – decisions which often go unmentioned in the manifestos – it is the Prime Minister's gut instincts which count. The pressures to solve problems and assuage demands by more public spending, intervention and controls can become almost irresistible – even for an instinctive free marketeer.

Mr Blair may believe with his head that government spending is not the universal panacea: but what about his heart – and, indeed, his gut?

In any case, government is not about generalities but about specifics. Only if you have the conviction – the Conservative conviction – that it is wrong to spend more taxpayers' money unless the reasons for doing so are overwhelming – and even if then you don't sleep easily after doing so – are you likely, as Prime Minister, to face down the pressure.

Suspicions that a Labour government would in practice become too soft a touch on public spending are compounded by all the misty talk about boosting communities and community values.

Now, communities can be sustained in two ways only – either by the state, which is what community politics, community leaders, community health, community housing, community centres and so on ultimately rely on.

Or communities can be based on genuine volunteers, sometimes local businesses, sometimes individuals with a common, freely chosen goal – like those who founded the great voluntary movements of the Victorian era which are still with us.

In some cases, to be sure, the state – often in the form of local government – can play a modestly useful part in 'community projects'.

But the risk is that community comes to mean collective; collective comes to mean state; and thus the state expands to replace individual effort with subsidised activism.

It is free, enterprising, self-reliant, responsible individuals that Britain needs. It's when we have more of them, that our communities will take better care of themselves.

But I believe there is a still more important reason why Labour should not be entrusted with government. They may protest that they are no longer socialists: but they have lost none of their zeal for constitutional upheaval.

The Labour Party's proposals on devolution threaten chaos, and possibly the dissolution of the Union of the United Kingdom itself.

Moreover, by embracing European federalism – through the European social chapter and, above all, the European single currency – a Labour government could deal a terminal blow to the traditions of British parliamentary democracy.

Cutting the state down to size
Traditionally, the socialists believed that the state must make people equal; though an honest look at the perks and privileges of the Communist *nomenklatura* might have set them right about that.

The new-look Labour Party now apparently wants the state to make people high-minded and socially aware; though a thought for how difficult the Churches find it to change people's behaviour ought to induce some doubts when mere politicians start to preach.

It seems to me that New Labour has a new song – one that was made famous by Dame Vera Lynn:

'Wishing will make it so
Just keep on wishing, and cares will go…
And if you wish long enough, wish strong enough
You will come to know
Wishing will make it so.'

But it won't – any more than you can make people good by legislation.

So the limitation of government is still the great issue of British politics – and indeed to a remarkable degree of global politics.

The threat to limited government did not end with the collapse of Communism and the discrediting of socialism. It remains an issue in Western – particularly European – democracies. There is a constant tendency, in which pressure groups, vested interests and the media play a part, for government to expand.

One of Thatcher's laws – for which I owe something to Lord Acton – is that all government tends to expand, and socialist government expands absolutely.

If you start with their view of the state – that it exists to right social wrongs rather than to create a framework for freedom – you can never find the definitive justification for saying 'no'. Above all, you cannot say 'no' to demands for more spending on welfare.

That is why in Sweden the share of national income the Government took reached some 70%. It's why it's several points higher in Europe on average than here. The dominant political philosophies of those countries have been Socialist, or

Social Democrat or Christian Democrat – all of them views which hold that the state, rather than individuals, is ultimately responsible for what happens in society.

This is in marked contrast to the United States which, even when the Democratic Party is in charge, has never been converted to the idea that government – let alone the federal government – has the right to intervene whenever it wants.

It is also in marked contrast to those Asia-Pacific countries – like Hong Kong, the Little Tigers and, of course, the mighty Japan – where government's share of GDP remains very low.

Spending at just over a third of GDP in the United States, and a quarter or less in the Asia-Pacific, has resulted in low taxes and high growth rates.

Their example, like that of Britain in the 1980s, shows what works – just as the over-spent and over-regulated Scandinavian model shows what does not.

It was with the best intent that post-war governments spent more on welfare, believing that as the standard of living rose, people would do more to look after themselves. What we had to do, as Keith often said in earlier years, was to break the 'cycle of deprivation'.

But the more we spent, the greater the dependency, illegitimacy and crime became. And of course the tax burden rose.

Western countries have now woken up to the problem. But they are still paralysed by it.

Here, though, Peter Lilley has been advancing steadily with social security reform, making important changes to reduce future burdens. Yet, as Peter himself often reminds us, social security still accounts for over 40% of central government spending and costs every working person £15 every working day.

Certainly, the proposals increasingly favoured by the Labour Party for a much higher compulsory second pension – paid for by much higher compulsory contributions – offer no way out.

It is one thing to encourage people to make provision for themselves, as we do with housing, health and pensions. It is also acceptable in some cases to ensure that people make some minimum contribution towards benefits, as we do through the National Insurance system.

But the Labour Party's plans would involve a large increase in compulsory saving which – as you would expect from them – results in a large decrease in personal liberty.

Alleviating the burden of the social security budget is a thankless but vital task, for which real Tory stamina is required. It will not be done by financial sleight of hand.

But the possibility of a really radical approach to spending, requiring large-scale removal or transferral of government functions, must also remain on the agenda.

Last November, a brilliant and provocative Centre for Policy Studies pamphlet by Patrick Minford – 'Public Spending: A 20-Year Plan for Reform' – reminded us how far we still might go, and how great the potential gains. The spending cuts he proposes would also lead to dramatic tax cuts – with a big impact on growth.

Whether Professor Minford's proposals are deemed acceptable or not, they are extremely valuable in illustrating the possibilities.

So I welcome the determination of the Chancellor of the Exchequer to bring public spending below 40% of GDP. And I hope that at the next election we will be equipped with plans to bring it down over a period of years by much more.

Limited government doesn't mean weak government, only less government.

This is shown by the courageous and far-reaching reforms which Michael Howard has been making in the criminal justice system. The strength of the opposition he faces from the vested interests shows he is right – almost as much as do the encouraging recent crime figures.

'Our new [European] masters'

But today the main challenge to limited government comes not from within these shores at all, but rather beyond them – from the European Union. There is, of course, also a challenge to self-government – and the two are closely connected.

The activity of the European Court, which can only ultimately be checked by amending the European Communities Act itself, is increasingly undermining our judicial system and the sovereignty of our Parliament.

Proposals are being made for common European defence – proposals which Michael Portillo has roundly and rightly attacked.

They too are a threat to national independence.

But most important, of course, is the proposed single European currency which, as John Redwood has argued, 'would be a major step on the way to a single European nation'.

The Prime Minister will have the support of all of us who wish to see these dangerous and damaging proposals resisted, and the present trends reversed, as he argues Britain's case at the forthcoming inter-governmental council. And we look forward to a successful outcome.

But vital as the issue of self-government is, it is limited government that concerns me today. For the European Union not only wishes to take away our powers; it wishes to increase its own.

It wants to regulate our industries and labour markets, pontificate over our tastes; in short to determine our lives. The Maastricht Treaty, which established a common European citizenship and greatly expanded the remit of the European Commission, shows the outlines of the bureaucratic superstate which is envisaged.

And Maastricht is the beginning, not the end of that process.

Indeed, we are increasingly seeing the emergence of a whole new international political class.

Some of them are politicians who have failed in their own countries, and so have tried their luck overseas.

Some are officials who understand nothing of our British distinction between the legitimate powers of the elected and those of the unelected.

Almost 50 years ago, the Conservative journalist Colm Brogan wrote an incisive critique of the post-war Labour government with its arrogant bossiness and intrusive cackhandedness. He called it *Our New Masters*.

The title is equally appropriate to the 'new European masters'.

And it is no surprise to me – as someone who always recognised the socialist destination of this Euro-federalist dream – that now the Labour Party welcomes it all so warmly.

What they can't achieve in an independent, free enterprise Britain, they can hope to secure in a Euro-federalist Britain, whose people's instincts are ignored and whose parliamentary institutions are over-ridden.

Self-government, limited government, our laws, our Parliament, our freedom.

These things were not easily won.

And if we Conservatives explain that they are now in peril, they will not be lightly surrendered.

In 'The Reeds of Runnymede', celebrating the signing of Magna Carta, Rudyard Kipling puts it like this:

'At Runnymede, at Runnymede,
Oh, hear the reeds at Runnymede:
You mustn't sell, delay, deny,
A freeman's right or liberty.
It wakes the stubborn Englishry,
We saw 'em roused at Runnymede!
… And still when Mob or Monarch lays
Too rude a hand on English ways,
The whisper wakes, the shudder plays,
Across the reeds at Runnymede.

And Thames, that knows the mood of kings,
And crowds and priests and suchlike things,
Rolls deep and dreadful as he brings
Their warning down from Runnymede!'

3 What was Thatcherism?

DOMINIC SANDBROOK

When Margaret Thatcher first walked into Downing Street as Prime Minister on 4 May 1979, she had already achieved something beyond any other post-war premier. She had been credited with her very own -ism: 'Thatcherism'. The irony, though, is that it had been coined by her opponents as a term of abuse. They invented the word 'Thatcherism' to describe what they saw as her right-wing fanaticism, which was supposedly out of step with the broad traditions of British political life.

Not surprisingly, therefore, she tried to discourage it. In her first major speech after becoming Tory leader, five years earlier, she had observed that 'to stand up for liberty is now called a Thatcherism', but dismissed it as one of Labour's 'tired and silly slogans'. And on the *Today* programme two years later, she again dismissed the idea of Thatcherism as an 'ogre', a 'ridiculous' idea invented by her opponents.[1]

The idea caught on, of course. Yet although some aspects are obvious – low taxes, free markets, a smaller state, strong defence – historians have never really agreed what Thatcherism was.

The most influential interpretation appeared in January 1979 in, of all places, *Marxism Today*. According to the cultural theorist Stuart Hall, Thatcherism was a kind of 'authoritarian populism – an exceptional form of the capitalist state', arousing public support by exploiting issues such as crime, race and education.

Soon other commentators weighed in with their own interpretations. Some saw it as the product of seminar rooms and think tanks, not least the Centre for Policy Studies; others as a transatlantic import, with Mrs Thatcher heading a British subsidiary of the American New Right.[2]

As the years passed, the arguments went on. Today, some historians see Thatcherism as an inevitable result of the decay of social democracy, others as a middle-class backlash against egalitarianism, still others as an unexpected product of the anti-establishment radicalism of the 1960s. Was it a revolutionary attack on the institutions that had underpinned the post-war consensus? Or was she actually *defending* that consensus against the militant left? Did it reflect a new stage in the evolution of industrial capitalism, or a new phase in the Cold War? Or was it the realisation of the free-market ideas of Friedrich Hayek and Milton Friedman? Was it about making the central government stronger? Or was it about weakening it? Was it, perhaps, all of these things at once? And if it was, does it really make sense to talk of Thatcherism at all?[3]

Was Thatcherism just Manchester Liberalism?

Among Mrs Thatcher's allies, many did believe there was such a thing as Thatcherism. The most articulate, the future Chancellor Nigel Lawson, famously described it as a 'mixture of free markets, financial discipline, firm control over public expenditure, tax cuts, nationalism, "Victorian values" (of the Samuel Smiles self-help variety), privatisation and a dash of populism'. And even Mrs Thatcher, having resisted the label for so long, eventually conceded that there was something to it. 'Sir Robin, it is not a name that I created in the sense of calling it an "ism",' she told *Panorama*'s interrogator Sir Robin Day in 1987. But then she went on:

'It stands for sound finance and Government running the affairs of the nation in a sound financial way. It stands for honest money – not inflation. It stands for living within your means. It stands for incentives because we know full well that the growth, the economic strength of the nation comes from the efforts of its people...

It stands for something else. It stands for the wider and wider spread of ownership of property, of houses, of shares, of savings. It stands for being strong in defence – a reliable ally and a trusted friend.

People call those things Thatcherism; they are, in fact, fundamental common sense and having faith in the enterprise and abilities of the people… That's all that Thatcherism is.'

It is a wonderfully revealing passage, but also a surprising one. Almost everything Mrs Thatcher said – honest money, living within your means, incentives, ownership, strong defence – could have been said by any Conservative leader since the dawn of time.

But what is most striking about her definition is its simplicity. The most important words come near the end: Thatcherism, she says, is just 'fundamental common sense'.[4]

Of course, not everybody saw it that way. To Sir Ian Gilmour, who served in Mrs Thatcher's Cabinet from 1979 to 1981, Thatcherism was merely '19th-century individualism dressed up in 20th-century clothes', the bastard offspring of 'Manchester Liberalism'. Even some of her allies agreed with him. Her friend Woodrow Wyatt, a former Labour MP who had swung well to the right, claimed that she was 'not a Conservative', but a 'radical making a revolution which horrifies many Conservatives'. The economist Friedrich Hayek, whose book *The Road to Serfdom* (1944) is often seen as a central influence on Thatcherite thought, described himself as a liberal and even wrote an essay entitled 'Why I am Not a Conservative'. And the other great idol of the free-market right, the American economist Milton Friedman, sounded a similar note. 'The thing that people do not recognize is that Margaret Thatcher is not in terms of belief a Tory,' he explained. 'She is a 19th-century Liberal.'[5]

It is true that, with her Methodist middle-class roots, free-market rhetoric and open distrust of the party establishment, Mrs Thatcher sometimes sounded like a Victorian Liberal. In 1983 she joked that 'if Mr Gladstone were alive today he would apply to join the Conservative Party'. But if she was really a Liberal, what had she been doing in the Conservative Party since 1943? Why did nobody notice?

The obvious answer is that she was saying nothing that most Conservatives did not themselves believe. Free-market liberalism had been part of their repertoire since Sir Robert Peel's day, while cutting taxes, rolling back the state and encouraging private enterprise had been Tory themes for decades. And if a true-blue Conservative leader such as Bonar Law or Stanley Baldwin had read Mrs Thatcher's party conference speeches, they would have agreed with almost every syllable.[6]

Of course, this contradicts the common view that Thatcherism was a revolution in British political economy, marking a great break between one era and another. It is certainly true that when she and Keith Joseph and their allies set up the Centre for Policy Studies, they believed they were doing something new, even something radical. Yet it is also telling that Mrs Thatcher never sought to dissociate herself from her party's history. 'All my predecessors – yes, I agree, Disraeli; yes, Harold Macmillan,' she told Robin Day. 'I would say I am right in their tradition.' Nigel Lawson said much the same. Was Thatcherism really 'some alien creed masquerading as Conservatism?' he wondered in 1980. 'I can only say that, as a Conservative, it feels pretty Conservative to me.' Yes, the Government sometimes invoked 'new sages – such as Hayek and Friedman'. But that was simply because these writers were 'reinterpreting the traditional political and economic wisdom of Hume, Burke and Adam Smith'. So what was so new about Thatcherism? 'In economic terms,' Lawson concluded, 'very little.'[7]

Was Thatcherism dogmatic?
One of the common misconceptions about Thatcherism, especially on the left, was that it was a fixed, coherent, 'neo-liberal' creed with clearly defined methods and principles. But this is nonsense. Thatcherism was

not a rigid, monolithic project. It was always fluid, always changing. In 1976 Mrs Thatcher had talked about standing up to the Soviet Union; in 1979 she emphasised taming the unions; by the end of 1984 her focus had already shifted to privatising the public utilities, which she had not even mentioned five years earlier. Some historians even think there was no one 'Thatcherism' but 'several different Thatcherite projects' competing for attention.

What is certain is that there was no blueprint, not even Hayek's *Road to Serfdom*, because Mrs Thatcher did not believe in blueprints. 'Vision, not blueprint; values and principles, not doctrines,' she told a Conservative audience in 1977. Even the word 'monetarism' rarely passed her lips. Instead she preferred to talk about 'sound money' and, of course, 'good housekeeping'.[8]

This was not just spin. Mrs Thatcher was a practical politician, not a political philosopher. As she herself told Michael Cockerell in 1979, she was guided by 'instincts and feelings', not doctrines or textbooks. This does not mean, of course, that she was a mere opportunist. Her principles were clear and unchanging: free markets, low taxes, law and order, strong defence, a horror of inflation and so on. So when, for example, she reflected on the creation of the CPS in a speech memorialising Sir Keith Joseph, she reached for very familiar vocabulary. Their goal, she said, was 'to redefine the principles and policies which would restore the richness of life by liberating the genius of the people and limiting the powers and role of government'.[9]

But like any successful politician, she was flexible about how she interpreted those principles. She liked winning elections; if that meant downplaying some elements or compromising on others, she was perfectly happy to do so. She usually hid this pragmatic side from the public, because she was worried it would make her look like Ted Heath in a dress. But her civil servants saw how she really worked. Her longest-serving Cabinet Secretary, Robert Armstrong, even remarked that he had never met a politician who was more skilful 'in combining rhetoric which was faithful to her principles with policies that were totally pragmatic'.[10]

The best way to think of Thatcherism, then, is not as a philosophical dogma but as a loose mixture of themes, instincts and attitudes, rooted in the soil of Middle England and the long history of the Conservative Party. As Alfred Sherman – her political adviser and the driving force behind the CPS – remarked, it had originated 'less as a doctrine than as a mood', defined by 'beliefs and values' rather than policies and pledges.

But it was also a product of a very particular historical moment, the late 1970s. And one principle, more than almost any other, underpinned everything Mrs Thatcher did: her belief that Britain was in deep national decline.[11]

Mrs Thatcher was not, of course, the first party leader to argue that Britain was going backwards. But none of her predecessors had been so passionate or so apocalyptic. Her first election broadcast, on 16 April 1979, put it centre stage:

> 'We can go on as we are. In a way that is the easy option. But we could not do that for long. Year after year we have been falling further behind friends and neighbours. And the British people will not indefinitely tolerate our country becoming the poor relation of Western Europe. If we go on declining, we shall sooner or later fall; and we shall become a quite different kind of country…'

She sounded the same note at her set-piece rallies, warning audiences that without change, 'our glories as a nation will soon be a footnote in the history books'. And when she talked to the BBC's Michael Cockerell a week before polling day, her voice almost cracked as she contemplated the nation's fortunes. 'I can't *bear* Britain in decline. I just can't,' she said earnestly. 'We who either defeated or rescued half Europe, who kept half Europe free, when otherwise it would be in chains! And look at us now!'[12]

Almost all Mrs Thatcher's allies shared her belief that the nation was in near-terminal crisis. Her future Press Secretary Bernard Ingham, formerly a keen Labour activist, said he had 'had enough of us being laughed at as a country'. Many of her colleagues saw things in even bleaker terms. Britain was charting 'a unique course', declared Sir Keith Joseph, 'as it slides from the affluent Western world towards the threadbare economies of the Communist bloc'.[13] Indeed, reversing this perceived decline was always one of the chief goals of the CPS. As Mrs Thatcher herself remarked in her later tribute to Joseph's work, it was 'by implementing the policies worked out by Keith and the Centre that we gradually restored the confidence and reputation of our country'.[14] But at the time, few gave her long odds of success. Indeed, many of her allies remained astonishingly pessimistic, in private as in public.

'We in the Western world have learned to live for today not tomorrow,' Sir Geoffrey Howe told Hugo Young. 'We are heading for a really terrible time unless we can reverse this trend… a kind of Romanian or other East European economy.' The next election, Nigel Lawson remarked in February 1979, was 'our last chance to rescue the British economy from the depressing spiral of decline'. Yet Thatcher herself was in no doubt. In her memoirs she quoted Pitt the Elder in 1756: 'I know that I can save this country and that no one else can.'[15] It was, she admitted, a 'presumptuous' comparison. 'But if I am honest, I must admit that my exhilaration came from a similar inner conviction.'[16]

What makes Mrs Thatcher's invocation of Pitt the Elder so revealing is that she is often thought to have been indifferent to the value of history. In fact, as Charles Moore's biography shows, she had an intensely romantic sense of history, which is why she took so much trouble getting pictures of Nelson and Wellington for No 10. When the South African writer Laurens van der Post interviewed her at the end of 1982, she took great delight in showing off not only Robert

Clive's Chippendale table, Pitt the Younger's desk and Churchill's chair but also a 'little scientific gallery' she had built up in the dining room, with pictures and busts of Humphrey Davy, Joseph Priestley and Isaac Newton. Warming to the historical theme, van der Post asked if she would have been a Roundhead or a Cavalier. 'I'd have been a Cavalier, a Royalist,' she said instantly.[17]

John Hoskyns, who worked with the CPS before moving into No 10 as part of Mrs Thatcher's new Policy Unit, thought that at heart she was driven by 'a patriotic impulse and a sense of shame about what had happened to our country'. Nobody who cared only for market values would have chosen 'I Vow to Thee, My Country' as her favourite hymn. No Roundhead revolutionary would have been so fond of pomp and pageantry. And what people often miss about Thatcherism is just how much she was inspired by her faith in Britain's exceptional history and unique destiny. 'Britain is not just another country; it has never been just another country,' she told Robin Day. 'We would not have grown into an Empire if we were just another European country with the size and strength that we were. It was Britain that stood when everyone else surrendered.' That last line is very telling. At the outbreak of the Second World War, she had been an impressionable 14-year-old. Even decades later, her voice thickened with emotion whenever she mentioned 'Winston'.[18]

Was Thatcherism political Methodism?

So was there *anything* distinctive about Thatcherism? There was, but it was a question of tone as much as content. When Ferdinand Mount went to see Mrs Thatcher about working in No 10, he was taken aback by her unapologetic earnestness. 'Education is only part of it,' she told him. 'What we really have to address are the values of society. This is my real task, to restore standards of conduct and responsibility.' Mount found all this 'both startling and thrilling'. After years of 'weary, professional cynicism', nothing had prepared him for 'the naked zeal, the direct, unabashed appeal to morality, the sheer seriousness' of her vision. Not since Gladstone, he thought, had there been a prime minister whose politics were so firmly anchored in what she called the 'real and absolute difference between right and wrong'.[19]

With all politicians, there is always a suspicion that they may not mean what they say. But Mrs Thatcher's moralism was absolutely genuine. The proof lies in the handwritten notes for her conference speeches, before her speechwriters polished them into something more conventional. The case for 'economic freedom', she scribbled in October 1979, was consistent with 'certain fundamental moral principles of life itself. Each soul and person matters. Man is imperfect. He is a responsible being. He has freedom to choose. He has obligations to his fellow men.' In a foreshadowing of her much-misunderstood remark that there was no such thing as society, she added: 'Morality is *personal*. There is no such thing as a collective conscience… To talk of social justice, social responsibility, a new world order may be easy but it does not absolve each of us from personal responsibility.' Her speechwriters cut the lot.[20]

Yet the public were left in no doubt about Mrs Thatcher's moralistic outlook. In her adoption speech at Finchley in 1979, she claimed that Britain's economic ills reflected a wider 'decline of manners, of morals, of shared beliefs'. Inflation, she told a service in 1981, was a 'moral issue, not just an economic one'. This was just not the kind of thing senior politicians said. Yet Mrs Thatcher insisted that Britain's decline was rooted in the fact that 'only a minority acknowledge the authority of God in their lives'. And although her speeches were not always so explicitly Christian, they almost always had a religious dimension. Again and again she reached for the language of the Sunday school. 'I am in politics because of the conflict between good and evil,' she told The Times in 1984, 'and I believe that in the end good will triumph.'[21]

Where all this came from is no mystery. As a child, Margaret Roberts had been brought up to say grace before every meal and to go to chapel four times on Sundays. Her father was a lay preacher, whose sermons insisted on the importance of hard work, clean living and individual salvation. And although she later moved away from Methodism to join the Church of England, she always drew inspiration from what she had heard on the hard wooden pews of Grantham. Indeed, it was the hard wooden pews of Grantham that gave Thatcherism its distinctive character. No modern party leader had ever talked so openly about virtue and vice, salvation and responsibility, freedom and servitude.

Some of her ministers found this embarrassing, but her admirers found it invigorating. For years they had been listening to left-wing speakers arguing that conservatism was merely a front for selfishness and wickedness. Now the boot was on the other foot. And this surely helps to explain the virulence of her critics' hatred. They were used to occupying the moral high ground; yet now they were facing somebody who said, entirely sincerely, that they were the agents of wickedness.[22]

Was Thatcherism populism?

Yet Thatcherism was more than just political Methodism. Indeed, although Mrs Thatcher relished talking about her faith, she was never more effective than when she took politics out of the chapel and into the home. Whenever she turned to the economy, for example, she instinctively talked in terms of good housekeeping and the family budget.

'I too know what it's like running a house and running a career. I know what it's like having to live within a budget. I know what it's like having to *cope*,' she told a studio audience in April 1979. And whenever her opponents accused her of ideological extremism, she had the perfect answer. 'My politics are based not on some economic theory,' she told the News of the World, 'but on things I and millions like me were brought up with: an honest day's work for an honest day's pay; live within your means; put by a nest-egg for a rainy day; pay your bills on time; support the police.' Who could disagree?[23]

The fact that those words appeared in the News of the World is very revealing. Mrs Thatcher was not the first prime minister to flirt with populism, but none had ever done it so vigorously. Her critics sneered that she had turned the party of estate owners into the party of estate agents; one historian has written that 'Thatcherism owed more to the Sun than the Spectator'.

But there were millions more Sun readers than Spectator readers, and an awful lot more estate agents than estate owners. As her strategist Gordon Reece told her, their goal was to reach the kind of people, especially women, who watched *Coronation Street* and *Top of the Pops*. And since this meant reaching across class lines, she talked not of working-class or middle-class people, but of 'ordinary people', the 'quiet majority' or 'ordinary working families'. Historians have calculated that between 1975 and 1990, she used the phrases 'ordinary people' or 'ordinary working people' at 175 different events.[24]

The idea of 'ordinariness' played a central part in the political culture of the 1980s. If nothing else, it was a clever way of appealing, in the same word, to middle-class and working-class voters alike. In Mrs Thatcher's moral universe, both groups were natural Conservatives. As ordinary people, they were decent, patriotic and respectable: they worked hard, owned their own homes (or wanted to), cherished their families and obeyed the law.

As she told a conference of Conservative trade unionists in 1978, there was nothing remarkable about being a Tory. They were simply 'a party of ordinary, commonsense, hard-working freedom-loving people'. Against them, though, was pitted a stuck-up, self-satisfied establishment of socialist politicians, trade union barons, left-wing teachers, militant students and rent-a-mob rabble-rousers. They did not understand good housekeeping. They did not love British history. They did not care about the nation's moral and economic decline. And they were not, of course, ordinary.[25]

The girl from Grantham

It was here that Grantham came in so handy. The Sun even called it 'the most boring town in Britain'. Not only was it literally in the middle of England, it was Middle England in microcosm. The young Margaret Roberts had been in no hurry to stay: after she left at the age of 18, she spent the rest of her life in the richer and more glamorous south, and never returned for more than a day or two. But once she became Conservative leader, Grantham became very useful. Every time she invoked the grocer's shop, the grammar school and the Methodist chapel, she reinforced the message that she was, in her own words, a 'plain straightforward provincial', just like the voters she was trying to reach.

No wonder, then, that she always insisted that she had learned her ideas in the Grantham grocer's shop. In her telling, the Lincolnshire market town in the 1930s was Eden before the Fall, a united, contented community where ordinary people worked hard, raised their families and went to church without worrying about inflation or strikes or students or subversives. This was the Britain she wanted to build, Grantham wreathed in glory.

And so on the steps of No 10, at the moment of supreme triumph, she did not forget the obligatory nod to her home town – or to her father, the self-made grocer and Methodist preacher from whom she had got all her ideas. 'Well, of course, I just owe almost everything to my own father. I really do,' she said seriously. 'He brought me up to believe all the things that I do believe and they're just the values on which I've fought the election. And it's passionately interesting to me that the things that I learned in a small town, in a very modest home, are just the things which I believe have won the election.'

It was the last thing she said, before she went in.[26]

What was Thatcherism?

Dominic Sandbrook is the author of several books about post-war Britain, most recently Seasons in the Sun and Who Dares Wins, which cover the late 1970s and early 1980s respectively. Formerly an academic historian, he is a columnist for The Times and book critic for The Sunday Times, and co-presents the world's most popular history podcast, The Rest is History.

4 Alfred Sherman and the Fanatical Lamas

CHARLOTTE HOWELL

In 1947 Antony Fisher, the founder of the Institute of Economic Affairs, asked Friedrich Hayek how best to resurrect liberal economics in Britain. Hayek immediately warned 'against wasting time… by taking up a political career'. As Fisher wrote, Hayek 'explained his view that the decisive influence in the great battle of ideas and policy was wielded by the intellectuals, whom he characterised as "the second-hand dealers in ideas"'.[1]

Even though politicians like Margaret Thatcher dominate our history books, their freedom of manoeuvre is often dictated – as Hayek said – by what 'set of beliefs' is generally accepted at the time.[2] The economic and trade union reforms achieved by Thatcher's governments in the 1980s would have seemed impossible just 10 years before. Who were the thinkers who gave Joseph and Thatcher the intellectual freedom and confidence to pursue their political instincts?

In 2007, Sir John Hoskyns told us to 'pay attention to Alfred Sherman' because he was right long before Joseph and Thatcher.[3] Indeed, from 1974 to 1979, there were three men who did more to invent 'Thatcherism' than anyone else: Sherman, Hoskyns and Norman Strauss. Their work at the Centre for Policy Studies was vital to Thatcher's success, but it is not often recognised with sufficient clarity.

Thatcher herself admitted later that 'I could not have become Leader of the Opposition, or achieved what I did as Prime Minister, without Keith. But nor, is it fair to say, could Keith have achieved what he did without the CPS and Alfred Sherman.'[4]

Who was Sir Alfred Sherman? And why is his role so often overlooked?

A Marxist mindset

In the summer of 1973, Keith Joseph was in a state of anguish. His sometime speechwriter, Alfred Sherman, had written a series of articles that were sharply critical not just of the Conservative Party, but Joseph himself. In the most brutal, 'Counting the Cost of New Towns', Sherman attacked Joseph's efforts as Minister for Housing in the 1960s: 'Zealots did not even stop to consider what makes old towns work… they held to naive determinist views which ignore the human element.'[5]

Joseph had always been sympathetic to the IEA's liberal economics, but repeatedly failed to implement the philosophy when in government. Years later, Joseph confirmed that Sherman's articles had 'spoilt [his] summer holiday'. But they also prompted him to begin thinking seriously about where Conservative policy had gone wrong in recent years.[6]

With characteristic greatness of spirit, he got back in touch with Sherman, as well as Alan Walters and Ralph Harris at the LSE and IEA. He was surprised by Walters' reaction: 'No, he didn't feel like shaking hands. How on Earth could a man of Joseph's intelligence have allowed himself to be party to the economic folly of the Heath Government?'[7]

From then on, at Joseph's invitation, the 'crackpot monetarists'[8] spent many evenings with him explaining what was wrong with the Conservatives' economic policy. Inspired and invigorated by their criticism, Joseph brought along a sympathetic colleague, Margaret Thatcher. He decided to create a new institute to propagate such thinking within Conservative circles. Enlisting the operational and financial help of Nigel Vinson, a successful businessman and key ally, the Centre for Policy Studies was born.

Joseph's decision that Sherman be the 'moving spirit' of the newly formed CPS was dangerous but brilliant. Sherman's story was a novelist's dream: the son of an East End Jewish Labour councillor who fought as a machine-gunner alongside Spanish Communists before taking a degree at LSE and working as a journalist.

Unimpressed by the realities of Communism while reporting from Yugoslavia, he transformed, with characteristic vigour, into a radical free marketeer. Famous for his aphorisms, he told Hoskyns: 'It's not what a man believes that matters, but what he takes for granted', and challenged the consensus view on everything from the money supply to mass tourism.[9]

Hoskyns remembered: 'There was always a new insight, an outrageous suggestion and a disconcerting conversational style. Someone would say that what we had to do was such and such. Alfred would cut in, "Who is 'we'?"'[10]

Sherman freely acknowledged the retention 'of his Marxist mindset',[11] arguing that 'there are enough pragmatists around – what Britain needs is men of conviction'.[12] He was regularly furious that no one seemed to understand the workings of 'cause and effect'[13] and constantly reminded politicians of the difference between 'popular policies on the one hand and policies that achieve popular results'.[14]

His greatest talent, however, was the ability to translate technical jargon into catchy phrasing; his articles and speeches command you to listen.

Less than 10 days after its formal foundation, Joseph's high-profile performance at Upminster was an early triumph for the CPS. The speech was packed with Shermanite idiom, including a *mea culpa* for Britain's economic stagnancy after '30 years of good intentions'.[15]

Joseph continued to make a series of high-profile outings throughout 1974. Eventually, just before the October election, the arch-Heathite Jim Prior was sent to ask Thatcher to stop Joseph from making the provocatively titled Preston speech, 'Inflation is Caused by Governments'. She replied: 'Oh, I don't know... I think Alfred has written it for Keith, and I think you'll find that Keith is most determined to make it.'[16]

The CPS archives contain the reworked drafts of many of these speeches. Each had an exhaustive preparation, with near-constant memorandums flying between Sherman, Joseph and Thatcher, tracing Sherman's guiding hand and relentless eye for detail.[17] Together, they were creating a new brand of conservatism – and the consensus Keynesians were not happy.

Battling the Tory establishment

The Keynesians had a useful ally in the shape of Chris Patten, who became head of the Conservative Research Department in the opposition years. Patten was an acolyte of Sir Ian Gilmour, the intellectual leader of the 'One Nation' collectivists and a notoriously 'wet' shadow minister.

Patten loathed Sherman and his team of 'dangerous radicals' at the CPS.[18] Ferdinand Mount commented in 1978 that the CRD was 'mostly devoted to the Keynesian, Butskellite, Macmillanish views of the age. And they do not take to new ideas any more readily than any other entrenched bureaucracy.'[19] In short, the CRD was staffed by aspiring parliamentary candidates who preferred a safe 'middle ground' to dangerous new ideologies.

As the shadow minister in charge of reviewing Conservative Party policy, Joseph had tried to inject excitement into the CRD repeatedly since 1974. Now, as Thatcher's chief front bench ally, he highlighted the unique 'chance to seize the intellectual initiative from the socialists'.[20] But all this inspired was greater collaboration between the CRD and Prior. In a letter to Patten in 1976, Joseph criticised the inadequacy of CRD work on unemployment statistics. Gerald Frost at the CPS was running a project to correct inaccurate data published by the Department of Employment and Joseph's letter chastised Patten for not recognising these corrections. He requested in unequivocal terms that 'the CRD's thinking on the subject should widen'.[21]

In April 1976 Joseph's series of speeches, drafted by Sherman, culminated in his legendary Stockton performance, 'Monetarism Is Not Enough'. Just before delivery Joseph sent a copy to Patten 'in case you might like to see it'.[22] As before, he decided to 'not circulate the full text through CCO [Conservative Central Office]' as unhelpful leaks were becoming increasingly common – the CRD would make every attempt to discredit CPS people and ideas.[23]

By 1976, a guerrilla war between the CPS and CRD was in full flow and an isolated Joseph was relying more and more on Sherman. Put simply, without the radical thinking and intellectual support of the CPS, he and Thatcher would never have been able to make the case for their new set of ideas.

Building alliances

Always on the lookout for allies, Sherman scoured newspapers' letters pages daily and contacted everyone from professors to small business owners. In August 1975, he spotted an article in the Financial Times about a presentation on the British economy by an old acquaintance called Terry Price. 'What is unusual about this familiar catalogue of complaints,' said the article, 'is Mr Price's insistence that they all connect up, through a great matrix of cause and effect.'[24] You can almost see Sherman's ears pricking up.

On 29 September 1975, he invited Price to lunch at the CPS. Price, previously a senior government scientist, brought along John Hoskyns, a charming Wykehamist soldier who'd recently sold his company. Just like Nigel Vinson, he was frustrated by the crisis facing Britain, and decided to devote his time to trying to rescue the nation from economic catastrophe.[25]

Price and Hoskyns had bonded over their similar attempts to map the systemic nature of Britain's ailing economy with 'cause and effect "wiring" diagram[s]'. Using a scientific approach, they were frustrated that no one in government seemed able to appreciate the complex yet predictable and reinforcing processes that were causing Britain's unstable stop-go economics.

After meeting Hoskyns and Price, and seeing their diagrams, Sherman scribbled an enthusiastic note to Joseph, saying he'd met 'two really brilliant people who are keen to help', and arranged a meeting two weeks later.[26] Within a month, he had introduced Hoskyns to Norman Strauss, an unorthodox executive from IBM whom Joseph had met via Samuel Brittan at the Financial Times.[27]

Strauss described himself to Thatcher as a specialist in propaganda and strategic communications.[28] In his 1976 CPS paper 'The Need for New Data', he wrote that the most 'profitable research for a marketing company nowadays is psychological research' – a field yet to touch the political world – and 'the few pieces of research [at the CRD] that I have seen do not go into this at all'.[29]

Seeing a symbiotic potential between Strauss' work on communications and Hoskyns' work on the economy, Sherman brought them together. 'Like most people meeting Norman Strauss for the first time, I could not make him out,' said Hoskyns, but a 'clever and sceptical top executive, who had used him as an adviser, once said to me: "When I read Norman's report, I realised that he had discovered as much about… this company in 24 hours as I had in five years."'

On one occasion a BBC interviewer, shocked by Strauss' criticisms of the Civil Service, protested: 'But with all this criticism, what do you feel about Civil Service morale?' 'Still too high,' Strauss replied, quick as a flash. Just like Sherman, he often pointed out facts hidden in plain sight, and was viewed with intense suspicion by most politicians and their officials.

Freedom of movement

As the battle against the CRD, CCO and the Shadow Cabinet raged on, the CPS continued to follow Hayek's advice 'that to have any hope of having radical policies accepted the climate of opinion had to be changed first'.[30] In 1977 Sherman reminded Joseph that the primary goal remained 'to extend the Government's freedom of manoeuvre'[31] and Hoskyns agreed: 'Once we are clear on what economic and industrial policies are needed the key question is "What political innovation is needed to remove the political constraints on government's freedom to pursue such policies?"'[32]

Sherman made use of his journalism contacts to push CPS ideas out into the world. Peter Jay and William Rees-Mogg at The Times cleared whole features to publish speeches drafted by Sherman and delivered by Joseph.[33] Celebrated economists like Brittan were invited to read them before delivery.[34] These networks of 'second-hand dealers in ideas' became integral to Thatcher's early performances. Before a television interview with Brian Walden in 1977, for example, Sherman advised: 'My talks with friends of friends suggest that he will be taking two or three main topics and probing in depth.' He drafted a script that is covered with Thatcher's scrawls and underlining.[35]

Thatcher gave this interview considerable attention in her memoirs, but only briefly mentioned Sherman as the character behind her 'vital advantages'.[36] However, others remember her early willingness to listen, which was particularly focused upon Sherman.[37] Hugo Young recounts a furious Jim Prior and other Shadow Cabinet ministers being kept waiting outside the leader's office while she pursued 'one of her countless dialogues with Sherman', only to enter and be rebuffed with the phrase, 'But Alfred says...'[38]

In 1977, after nearly two years of prevarication and delay, during which Hoskyns almost walked away, Thatcher asked him and Strauss to produce a major strategy document in the wake of the IMF bailout. The crisis had arrived, and it was the time for radical ideas. 'Stepping

Stones' was straightforward and honest about the scale of the challenge – and the devastating consequences of failure. It spoke urgently, saying 'there is never a convenient time for strategic thinking… yet many of today's pressures are often themselves caused by a lack of strategy.'[39]

The report listed four key 'turnaround policies', most of which were dependent on curtailing union powers: currency stabilisation; shifting personal tax from income to expenditure; deregulating the private sector; and using North Sea Oil revenue to 'cut public sector borrowing'.

The report made clear 'there is nothing to gain… and everything to lose' by a 'low risk' approach, and that 'risks have to be taken if attitudes are to be changed'.[40] It argued that 'the Tories must engage with the unions in mature debate', and thereby cause voters 'to dislike them so intensely that their fear turns to anger about it'. Using simple language and common sense, Hoskyns and Strauss provided a comprehensive and scientific strategy. Apparently, Thatcher's 'eyes lit up' when she saw it.[41]

Even before 'Stepping Stones' was published, however, the CPS was already inciting a sense of crisis, on the basis that the UK required a shock to jolt it from its Keynesian rut. Inevitably, this approach caused a major disagreement with CCO. The central party protested that 'the public does not need convincing that the party is capable of embarking on a programme of dynamic action but rather that its dynamism will not capsize the boat'.[42]

Yet with 'Stepping Stones' as its guide, the CPS now doubled down on its strategy. Sherman strongly agreed with Hoskyns and Strauss that 'without a mood of desperation… the general public would have never countenanced such a vigorous new broom'.[43]

A private army

At a time of seemingly existential peril for the nation, those who supported Sherman argued that his lack of social grace was not only a fair 'price to pay to release his energies overall'[44] but a vital shield against friendly fire: if Sherman did the arguing, he could take the flak.

As Mount later wrote, 'he was right about a lot of things, and was never forgiven for it'.[45]

In the CPS's early months, Adam Ridley had been asked by Heath to keep an eye on the monetarists at the CPS and he wrote to Heath describing Sherman's credo as 'awkward'.[46] Thatcher agreed whole-heartedly, affectionately calling him 'the leader of the awkward squad'.[47] She was delighted by 'his complete disregard for other people's feelings or opinion of him', adopting it herself: 'If you just set out to be liked, you will be prepared to compromise on anything at anytime, and would achieve nothing.'[48]

With the tireless enthusiasm of a radical convert, Sherman fused nationalist populism and complex economic theory into the strident political voice we recognise as 'Thatcherism'. He refused to see the application of market theory and traditional Tory pragmatism as ideologically exclusive, prefiguring many of Thatcher's most famous sentiments: 'Self-interest is not enough… without patriotism, civic courage, a sense of obligation to family and fellow-men no society can flourish or even survive in the long run' – a realisation that 'an economy consists of people': the market is the beginning not the end.[49]

On a huge range of topics, from the early mutterings against a 'classless society' to Thatcher's lauded performances in Zurich (1977) and Madrid (1978), the CPS became Thatcher's schoolroom, and Sherman the tutor. She wrote to him after her 1977 Party Conference speech: 'There is no way I can thank you adequately, but I hope you know how much your work is appreciated.'[50] His enormous breadth of reading and intellectual clarity encouraged her to embrace her political instincts; he was the head to her heart.

While Sherman's accusation that CRD was actively working against its leader sounds conspiratorial, Mount is categorical in his corroboration. He agreed that when Sherman started snarling around Westminster, saying 'Margaret is surrounded by enemies', he was 'speaking nothing less than the truth'.[51] Sherman himself liked to distinguish between Thatcher's 'enemies' (in her own party) and 'opponents' (in the other parties), knowing that a war on the home front was worst of all.

The attacks against what The Guardian called the 'Potala of monetarism manned by fanatical lamas (a reference to the Tibetan temple)'[52] were relentless, vicious and sometimes hysterical.[53] In June 1978, The Times wrote: 'Why (it is asked) does Mrs Thatcher need her own policy research department when other leaders have been content with the Conservative Research Department? Who, anyway, is Alfred Sherman in Conservative politics? Why has he a hot line to Mrs Thatcher in Flood Street, Chelsea or the Commons that is not available to (say) Mr Whitelaw, Mr Francis Pym, or Mr James Prior?'[54]

In response, Sherman would mock the 'Conservative ranks… brandishing quotations from Burke, whom they revere the more for never having actually read'.[55] The reality, he said, was that CRD was 'doing little thinking on longer-term policy questions; its resources appear almost entirely pre-empted in servicing the day-to-day Parliamentary activities of Shadow ministers'.[56]

Electoral endgame

Contrary to some accounts of the period, the archives show that both Joseph and Thatcher remained reliant on Sherman throughout the 1979 election – and beyond. In 1978, Sherman wrote a series of confidential memos to Thatcher arguing that the time had come to take on the trade unions: 'The Unions' moral ascendancy has been eroded, they are no longer seen as valiant fighters for the underdog but as selfish and often ruthless operators.'[57]

'Stepping Stones' had been clear that 'there is one major obstacle – the negative role of the trade unions. Unless a satisfying and creative role can be developed, national recovery will be virtually impossible.'[58] Hoskyns, Strauss and Sherman worked together to argue that union reform must be the highest priority in government because without it, nothing else was possible. CPS speeches warned that this was 'our last chance to rescue the British economy'; that each vote was not just for a party but for a way of life.[59] With fury, Sherman lambasted 'middle-ground' escapism that failed to tackle the unions head on, and consensus solutions that ignored political history, economic theory and experience, contrasting it with the shared values, aims and aspirations of a unifying 'common-ground'.

All these preparatory briefing notes and strategy papers culminated in Thatcher's election broadcast on 30 April 1979: 'The decision is crucial. The problems facing Britain today are very grave.'[60]

After the election in 1979, Lord Thorneycroft, the Chairman of the party, received a letter from CRD complaining that though the leader's speeches were a great success, 'we were acutely conscious that no senior member of CRD was involved in their drafting and that we did not have the opportunity to vet final texts'.[61] The Sunday Times headlined its coverage: 'All of a Sudden Margaret Thatcher Looks Like a Real Prime Minister', but pointed out that such 'oratorical triumphs do not spring out of thin air'.[62]

The newspapers were right. For months her personal team of speechwriters at the CPS, including Sherman and Hoskyns, had met every day at 11am to debate how best to win over the elusive floating voter. Together, they had decided she must engage in 'not slamming but serious, destructive argument, clear and courteous. Humble, yet inspiring – Voice of future P.M.'[63]

Truth to power?
After the election victory, Hoskyns headed up the No 10 Policy Unit and took Strauss with him on a two-year loan from IBM, while Walters became special economic adviser to the Prime Minister in 1981. Sherman himself was in and out of Downing Street as and when he pleased.

Later in her life, Thatcher would pay tribute to Sherman, Hoskyns and Walters' contributions to her achievements as leader of the party and Prime Minister. However, in the early years of her government, like any politician, she was soon swamped by 'civilising' officials who were thrilled to take revenge on the 'awkward squad' at the first opportunity.

In the blink of an eye, Thatcher had transformed from an opposition leader unpopular within her own party into a magnet of power. Sherman knew well the dangers of the Civil Service in particular and had written countless briefings for Thatcher and Joseph on the importance of 'private armies' of advisers to counter its influence. Unfortunately, it was a priority that was – and still is – overlooked.

By 1981, Hoskyns had become frustrated by a lack of strategy and action from the Prime Minister. He told Thatcher and Joseph that he intended to resign. In his memoir, he says that when Joseph asked about Civil Service reform, an original CPS priority that remained untouched, he replied: 'What's the point, Keith?... A real "Stepping Stones" was not possible if the "client" was not willing to set aside even an afternoon to think about it.'[64]

At the time of Hoskyns' departure, Sherman was also facing problems at the CPS. Since 1979, his friend the historian Hugh Thomas had been helping with CPS speech-drafting for Thatcher, and had then become the think tank's Chairman. By 1983, internal priorities had begun to clash violently. Thomas was uncomfortable with Sherman's fundamentalist approach to intellectual independence and wanted to maintain a cosy closeness with the new Government.

In October 1983, Thomas wrote to Sherman announcing new CPS terms of reference: it was to be 'a research body at the disposal of the Prime Minister and other Ministers with friendly relations with all levels of the Party'.[65] Sherman responded with unwavering clarity: 'The whole point of the Centre lay in its commitment to ideas and policies without committing the party leadership... It is precisely because the Centre and I did not commit the Party leaders that we were able to move the frontiers of debate and policy search within which the Conservative leaders are bound to operate… If the Centre can only do the Party's job, it becomes redundant.'[66]

It is perhaps inevitable that the radicals who pave the way to power are somewhat less convenient inside the palace gates. But the traditional interpretation that Sherman was just 'too difficult' to stay in post at his own creation is contradicted by much of the evidence. He was certainly a rebarbative personality. But appreciative of his relative unimportance, and how busy the Prime Minister was, he preferred that 'she should be spared the details' of his conflict with Thomas. And until May 1983 he continued to hope that his 'deliberately self-denying ordinance, never to discuss Centre affairs with the Prime Minister, will not bring decreasing returns'.[67] For all his intelligence and clarity about the Civil Service, Sherman sometimes showed a childlike naivety about how far officials and advisers with a nose for power will go to dispense with their rivals.

In just a few months, Thomas won the battle for the CPS. Unable to work freely, Sherman went on sabbatical, never to return. CPS study groups that had been a hotbed of radical thinking found themselves attracting careerists whose chief vocation was to climb the ladder of Conservative politics. Discussions that might inconvenience the Government were shut down. Even though the CPS went on to do valuable work on fleshing out the bones of economic reform, in particular in making the case for privatisation, the intellectual counter-revolution had come to an end.

By the end of her first term, Thatcher had lost the unique group of characters who had done more to further her career and save Britain from economic crisis than anyone. Sherman, Hoskyns and Strauss spoke truth to power, sought no sinecures and often worked for nothing because they 'cared passionately about the country'.[68] They were, in short, 'temperamental[ly] incapable of going native in Whitehall culture'.[69]

As anyone who has observed the animals of Westminster up close will agree, the 'fanatical lamas' were a rare breed indeed.

Charlotte Howell is the founder of Xavier Britain, which specialises in bespoke fine bone china and luxury British tableware, and has written academically on the history of the Centre for Policy Studies. Previously, she worked in the Brexit team at Downing Street, as a speechwriter for Michael Gove MP and at Vote Leave.

5 Present at the Creation

ANTHONY SELDON

'Would you like to work at a new think tank over your summer holidays?' my father asked.

'What's it do?' I responded, possibly a little ungraciously.

'Well, it's like the IEA.'

'So how's it different?'

'Well…' he replied, and here I sensed he was struggling a bit. 'It's more focused on the short term and more overtly political. The IEA is more academic and research-based.'

'Does it have a name yet?'

'The Centre for Policy Studies, I think. Early days.'

'I'll give it a think, Dad,' I responded, replacing the phone in the JCR bar.

It was June 1974, and I was just finishing my first summer term studying PPE at Worcester College, Oxford. It was a time of palpable excitement, with change in the air. The defeated Tory prime minister, Edward Heath, was clinging on to the leadership, just. But intellectually, fresh currents were blowing up the River Thames from London towards Oxford.

'Do you share your father's politics?' I'd been asked at the entrance interview (you could ask such questions then). 'I'm not sure I know what his politics are,' I replied, disingenuously. But I went on to talk with relish about the 'new right' and how it differed from the 'old right'. The panel looked at me with a barely concealed scepticism.

My father, Arthur Seldon, had been one of the co-founders of the Institute of Economic Affairs back in 1955. But even though he was one of the leading voices of this 'new right', it was still not a movement that was explicitly identified with the Conservative Party. In February 1974 I'd returned to my parents' home in Sevenoaks to help campaign for the Liberals in the general election – since they were the party with which the family most identified.

At the time, it was clear that the tide was running out for Heath and his corporatist solutions to Britain's deep-seated economic woes. But Heath was unable to form a Con–Lib coalition government, so Harold Wilson and Labour came to power in early March. It rapidly became clear that they no more had the answers than when in office in the mid to late 1960s.

Meanwhile, my head was increasingly abuzz with ideas coming out of the IEA: William Niskanen with his politics of bureaucracy (anticipating the contemporary critique of Whitehall), Max Hartwell and his 'great debate' on poverty (anticipating the controversies over wokeism), and philosopher Karl Popper with his evergreen call to challenge nostrums and received wisdom. Increasingly, the conventional opinion in the mid-1970s was that the post-war consensus on the economy, which had prevailed since Clement Attlee had been Prime Minister 30 years before, had clearly failed. But what was to take its place?

A great time it was for anyone interested in ideas – and, indeed, to be setting up a new think tank.

Why was I asked to become an intern? I've no idea. But on 20 May, the CPS had held its inaugural management committee meeting, and they seem to have thought interns might do some donkey work at a time when funds were short. My father was friendly with the founding fathers of the CPS. Perhaps having his son on board might even seal a dynastic accord between these two free-market bodies?

In this new political climate, not totally unlike today, people were looking for fresh solutions. People were starting to take note of the IEA, which had been consistently disregarded by the economic and media mainstream since its founding less than 20 years before.

Still, the IEA was overtly academic, more a high table where erudite events were held and scholarly papers published than a marketplace where ideas were traded and sold. And very definitely not a campaigning body. So the case for an institution to galvanise, channel and persuade opinion-formers and politicians was demonstrably clear.

I was up for it.

'Yes, I'll do it!' I phoned my father to say two weeks later. 'Oh, will I get paid?'

I never did find out. In mid-June I met up with Simon Webley, one of the CPS's founders, who told me about the head honchos: Keith Joseph (Chair), Margaret Thatcher (Deputy Chair) and Nigel Vinson (Treasurer). He told me that the *eminence grise* (I had no idea what that meant) was an ex-Communist who fought in the Spanish Civil War, Alfred Sherman – the Dominic Cummings of the day.

'Sounds great,' I said. 'He's weird, but a visionary,' said Simon. 'Better still! And what will I be doing?' I never found that out either.

Monday, 1 July 1974, was when I pitched up at the premises at 8 Wilfred Street SW1, whose keys were handed over to the CPS that very morning. In a quiet Georgian street straight out of Jane Austen, yards away from the flower-festooned Cask and Glass pub (still there today), it was everything I romantically imagined a London office might be.

From the first moment, it was delightfully *ad hoc*. No one had a clue about anything, including who was to work in what room. Presiding over it all with elegant calm was the suave Deputy Director, Martin Wassell. But the force of nature was the Secretary, as she was called, Julia Scott-Barrett. Impossibly glamorous and commanding, she had everyone eating out of her hands. When she produced a bottle of Moet et Chandon champagne out of nowhere for my birthday, I thought life could get no better than this.

But what of the work? The pace certainly hotted up when we had periodic visitations from Keith Joseph – who shot off to a room upstairs. We were constantly expecting Margaret Thatcher, still six months from becoming party leader but clearly the figure to watch. She was certainly in constant contact with Keith and Alfred, but rarely came by – though when she did, we sensed her aura. Nigel Vinson was the avuncular presence, interested in everyone and everything, and as always, totally down to earth. He has become a lifelong friend, and was a wonderful support to me when I was Vice-Chancellor of the University of Buckingham, of which he has been a mainstay.

The principal research activities that I was engaged in were preparing material for two speeches given that summer by Keith Joseph, one on 8 August at Leith entitled 'Inflation is Decapitalising British Industry', and another at Preston on 5 September, entitled 'Inflation is Caused by Governments'. Milton Friedman had already declared that 'inflation is always, and everywhere, a monetary phenomenon', but the practical implications for government were still being worked out.

This was a critical task for the new right insurgents challenging Heath's statist approach. My job was to research facts for the speeches, including industrial and economic performance across Europe. The eminent lawyer Jonathan Sumption was the other researcher, infinitely more adept at the task than me. I still remember with shame that some of my research on socio-economic groupings for the Preston speech was plain wrong.

Liz Truss was born in Oxford the following year. I often think of this when writing a book about her now. She was so like Thatcher in many ways: but why did she not learn more from her about how to introduce change and take people with her?

What remains with me over the 50 years? I quit in late August 1974 to start preparing for the new university term, several weeks before the CPS's planned official opening on 1 November. But even in those earliest of days, I had a sense of being in at the beginning of something special. Of being caught up in the world of some magnetic minds, above all Thatcher and Joseph (then still deciding which one should challenge Heath).

Finally, the sense of a subversive and even mischievous enterprise – of a body that, even though it didn't fully know how in these anarchic first weeks, was consciously on a course that would shortly change history.

Sir Anthony Seldon is one of Britain's leading contemporary historians, educationalists and commentators, and the author or editor of over 45 books on contemporary history, including six books on recent prime ministers. Vice-Chancellor of the University of Buckingham from 2015 to 2020, he is currently head of Epsom College.

6 Did Monetarism Work?

TIM CONGDON

The economic policies of Margaret Thatcher, then and at the time, were presented as a dangerous innovation. The Centre for Policy Studies, from which many of those policies emerged, was accused by The Guardian of being a 'Potala of monetarism manned by fanatical lamas'. But the key to understanding that emblematic policy of monetarism is that it was not revolutionary at all. For Thatcher, Joseph and others – myself included – it was above all a restoration of a lost tradition.

In the 18th and 19th centuries, Britain was the home of classical liberalism. Admittedly, the phrase has more than one potential meaning, but it certainly included such notions as the freedom of the individual under the law and respect for private property. Thatcher and Keith Joseph were unusual politicians, in that they both had a strong and lively interest in political ideas, even – dare one say? – in political philosophy. They certainly believed that Britain's classical liberalism had contributed to its historical achievement.

So when they set up the Centre for Policy Studies in 1974, they wanted – as freedom-loving Conservatives – to restore a tradition of political thinking and practice, and to make it relevant to the future. I was lucky, as a young economist at the start of my career, to help in the Centre's work updating and refreshing this heritage. A central part of the agenda was to defeat inflation and to stabilise the public finances. I advocated, in particular, control over growth of the quantity of money and systematic reductions in the budget deficit, a policy approach which came to be known as 'monetarism'.

In a classically liberal society, the state's tasks were limited to defence and the provision of law and order, while key functions of the law were to define and protect private property. In a society of this kind, freedom in the economic sphere was, above all, freedom from government intervention. As Adam Smith explained in his 1776 *Wealth of Nations*, prices should be set by supply and demand in what he termed 'a system of natural liberty'. Were such 'natural liberty' to prevail, the state would have little to do.

Emphatically, the role of the state was not to meddle in the setting of wages and prices by private agents. All the same, it was supposed to honour its financial promises. In particular, the Government's bank – the Bank of England – was to ensure that the value of the pound sterling was to be kept stable relative to that of gold. This arrangement was part of a larger commitment to public morality and economic stability, with the Government's own budget to be balanced or in a small surplus.

Through the 20th century, classical liberalism went into retreat, in Britain as elsewhere. The leaders of thought and opinion moved towards 'the left', where the extreme left was represented by Marxism. According to Marx in his 1848 *Communist Manifesto*, the ultimate destination of all polities was Communism, when

> 'Society will take all forces of production and means of commerce, as well as the exchange and distribution of products, out of the hands of private capitalists and will manage them in accordance with a plan based on the availability of resources and the needs of the whole society. In this way, most important of all, the evil consequences which are now associated with the conduct of big industry will be abolished. There will be no more crises…'

'Crises' meant here the cyclical crises, the boom–bust cycles already evident in the mid-19th century when Marx was writing.[1] He recommended that in the Communist 'new social order', money – like the institution of private property – would be abolished. Cyclical crises could not then be caused by the antics of the banking system, and related upheavals in credit and money.

The emergence and failure of the post-war economic consensus
References to Karl Marx may seem anachronistic and rather shrill in the early 21st century, but matters were different 50 years ago. By the 1960s and early 1970s the leftward shift of elite thinking had created an existential problem for the many British traditions and institutions which had originated in the liberal culture of earlier centuries. One aspect of this problem was serious economic failure.

The growth of national output had through the post-war years been slower than in other advanced countries. The Conservative government of 1970–4, under Edward Heath as Prime Minister, with Anthony Barber as Chancellor of the Exchequer, engineered a big boom in 'a dash for growth'. But in 1974, when the CPS began, it was clear that the boom had provoked rapid inflation and would be followed by a bust. In the year to August 1975, the retail price index rose by 26.9%, the highest number in peacetime history. Indeed, the pound's loss of value in that one year was more than had been typical in the lifetimes of British people in the Hanoverian and Victorian eras.

Why had so much gone wrong with British economic policy-making? The leftward shift of high-level opinion had undoubtedly affected Britain's economists in the middle decades of the 20th century. Many of those approaching their career peaks had reached adulthood or were in their early career in the 1930s and during the Second World War. They had been saddened and alienated by the sorry spectacle of the American economy in the Great Depression of the early 1930s; they were impressed, by contrast, with the much-trumpeted and widely believed-in triumph of Soviet planning at the same time,[2] and by Russia's contribution to the Allied victory in the Second World War.

In the immediate post-war decades, most British economists believed in 'planning'. Taken to its logical conclusion, the state was to specify production targets for particular sectors, and to direct the allocation of labour and capital accordingly. Some prominent figures – notably Joan Robinson, variously associated in her career with Girton College, Newnham College and King's College at Cambridge, and a fellow of the British Academy from 1958 – were indeed Marxists. A clear majority of the economics profession despised money and monetary policy. Even if they did not go as far as Marx in recommending that the use of money be forbidden, they scoffed at once standard views on the role of money in the inflationary process. In a book on the British economy in the 1950s, Charles Kennedy, who was an economics don at Queen's College, Oxford, from 1948 to 1961, described the quantity theory of money as a 'doctrinal monster, which one [had] thought and hoped [was] extinct'.[3]

The best way to deal with inflation – in Kennedy's view and that of hundreds of other university economics teachers – was for the Government to set limits on increases in wages and prices, regardless of any resulting microeconomic inefficiency. The free market was scorned as ineffective and old-fashioned. Like sound money and a balanced budget, it was mocked as other fuddy-duddy Victorian orthodoxies had been in the early 20th century by Lytton Strachey and the rest of the Bloomsbury Group.

Any reference to the Bloomsbury Group of course raises the subject of one of its members – John Maynard Keynes, who is often regarded as the greatest economist of all time.

A discussion of Keynes' role in British policy thinking and making is complex because he was something of an intellectual chameleon. In any case, his successors – particularly a number of self-described

'Keynesians' at Cambridge University (who included Nicholas Kaldor and Richard Kahn as well as Mrs Robinson) – propounded a set of doctrines which they claimed would have carried Keynes' imprimatur.

The Cambridge Keynesians of the 1950s and 1960s thought that the Government's job was to secure full employment by the management of aggregate demand, where the management of aggregate demand involved variations in government spending and taxation, and hence in the budget balance. An increase in the budget deficit stimulated demand, according to the Cambridge Keynesians and their many acolytes; a reduction in the deficit reduced it.

Kaldor – like Kennedy – was dismissive of monetary policy and rude about the quantity theory of money. Adjustments to the budget balance constituted 'fiscal policy', and fiscal policy was to have pride of place in macroeconomic strategy and action.

And so we come back to the Heath–Barber boom of the early 1970s. At the Bretton Woods conference of 1944, Britain agreed to participate in the post-war system of fixed exchanges rates. This system was ostensibly a dollar standard, but the risk of inflationary policies in the United States of America was cramped by its obligation to redeem official dollar liabilities in gold at a fixed price of $35 an ounce.

In 1971 the USA broke the link with gold, and in 1971 and 1972 the United Kingdom moved, with many other countries, to float its exchange rate. From 1945 to 1971 the Bretton Woods system had imposed an external constraint on fiscal and monetary irresponsibility in the UK. The breakdown of the system removed this constraint.

The Keynesians took the opportunity to go on the rampage. From late 1971, macroeconomic policymaking became wildly expansionary. The 1972 Budget increased the budget deficit by over £3 billion, the equivalent of 5% of gross domestic product. The need to finance the deficit partly from the banking system, in conjunction with overdue measures of financial liberalisation and an associated surge in bank credit, led to an explosion in the quantity of money. Money growth on the then widely tracked M3 measure was 26.8% in the year to the fourth quarter 1972 and 27.1% in the year to the fourth quarter 1973.[4]

In other words, the quantity of money soared by over 60% in a mere two years. This pace of money expansion caused dramatic rises in asset prices and a vigorous upturn in aggregate demand. As so often in these cycles, asset price inflation spread to product and labour markets, and inflation at factory gates and in the shops started to accelerate.

On 6 November 1972 Heath announced an immediate freeze on all increases in wages and prices. According to the BBC in an 'On This Day' history comment, the 'controls on income and expenditure' were introduced 'after talks between the government, the Trades Unions Council and the Confederation of British Industry... failed to produce an anti-inflationary deal'. In a statement to the House of Commons, 'Prime Minister Edward Heath told MPs the government had decided to bring in laws enforcing... controls.'[5]

The Heath–Barber boom was Keynesianism run amok. But the intellectual context must be remembered. A clear majority of those economists with influence on the government of the day believed *both* that fiscal policy was the best tool for managing aggregate demand, with growth ambitions justifying so-called 'expansionary fiscal policy', *and* that inflation could be controlled – quite properly and very effectively – by the enactment of laws against it. Moreover, their assessment was that these laws would work regardless of the rate of money growth. After all, the quantity theory of money was an extinct doctrinal monster, wasn't it?

The 1981 Budget and overturning the economic consensus

After coming down from Oxford in summer 1973, I started my first job – on the economics staff of The Times – in October 1973.[6] My main tasks were reportage, to write news stories on the monthly statistics which reflected the shambles of the UK economy and its policymaking, as well as daily summaries of the gilt and money markets, and the foreign exchanges. But of course I had views on the major economic developments and what might be done to improve the situation.

My direct boss, Peter Jay, had already warned that 'the Barber boom' would end in a bust and was even worried that out-of-control inflation threatened Britain's democratic way of life.[7] One of his friends was Samuel Brittan, who was the main economics columnist on the Financial Times for much of the period from 1966 to his retirement in 2014. Both had met and come to admire Milton Friedman, the main supporter of the quantity theory of money in the late 20th century. For a few years Brittan and Jay were known as 'the monetarist twins', or even 'the terrible monetarist twins', because of their preparedness to cite money growth changes in their critiques of official policymaking.

I was influenced by these two brilliant and outstanding commentators. But I had done much reading on my own both before and during my four years at Oxford. I had, for example, dipped into Keynes' 1923 *Tract on Monetary Reform* and his 1931 volume of collected journalism, *Essays in Persuasion*. They showed me that Keynes was an admirer of market mechanisms, who wanted people to enjoy a private sphere and freedom of choice, and who deplored Marxism and the Soviet Union. I also could not fail to notice that the index of his 1936 *General Theory* had a mere two references to 'fiscal policy', but 26 to 'money, quantity of' and six to 'money, quantity theory of'.

It seemed to me that the Cambridge Keynesians were involved in dishonest fabrication. They purported to have the right to mint ideas as if they were Keynes', but their real game was intellectual counterfeiting. I wrote an article for the April 1975 issue of Encounter magazine in protest against their practices.

As described elsewhere in this essay collection, Alfred Sherman was instrumental in establishing the Centre for Policy Studies with Sir Keith Joseph, and was its first Director. He contacted me about my

Encounter article, and invited me to participate in CPS study groups and to publish under the CPS banner. I agreed to write a pamphlet called 'Monetarism: An Essay in Definition'. We deemed this to be worthwhile, as many people were not sure what monetarism meant. The pamphlet duly appeared in 1978, in both soft and hard covers, with the hard covers apparently causing some in-house controversy over cost. (I was a conceited young man who wanted to be able to say he had written a book. There are worse offences against good taste.)

The pamphlet was well timed, and had a worthwhile impact on the debates of the late 1970s and early 1980s. Politicians and journalists even used the phrase 'Thatcherite monetarism' to define the economic agenda of the Conservative government elected in 1979.

This agenda was undoubtedly very different from that of the 1970–4 Heath government. Prices and incomes policies backed by the law were dropped as a means of combating inflation. Instead the job was to be done by monetary restraint. Fiscal policy was subordinated to a money target regime formalised from 1980 in a 'Medium Term Financial Strategy (MTFS)'.

Along with such notables as Alan Budd and Terry Burns of the London Business School, I had for some years favoured an MTFS programme with quantified forward numbers on money growth and the budget deficit.[8] And it was the existence of the MTFS that led to perhaps the most contentious episode in British economic policy-making, the 1981 Budget.

Partly because a recession dented tax revenues and increased certain kinds of public expenditure, projections in early 1981 were for the budget deficit to be well above the figure envisaged in the MTFS. To maintain credibility, the then Chancellor of the Exchequer – Sir Geoffrey Howe, later Lord Howe – decided that taxes should be increased in order to keep the deficit within the prescribed limits.

This seemed to breach textbook Keynesian economics, which said that taxes should be cut and the deficit raised in a recession. Two economics professors at Cambridge University organised a letter to The Times to condemn the Budget decisions, and indeed monetarism, and managed to secure the signatures of 364 university teachers of economics.

Here was an outright and very public confrontation between the predominantly Keynesian university-based UK economics profession and the 'Thatcherite monetarists'. On the face of it, the contest was very uneven, as the monetarists were markedly fewer in number, and often – like myself – mere journalists or worked in the City of London.

The outcome of the confrontation may itself still be controversial. All the same, the 364 were wrong in one crucial respect. They forecast that the fiscal contraction – as they saw it – would lead to an intensification of the economic downturn. On the contrary, in the weeks following their letter the economy began to show signs of recovery. Roughly trend growth was sustained for a few quarters, while 1984 enjoyed above-trend growth.

Another weakness of the letter was its assertion that 'alternative policies' were available, without saying what they were. If the 364 understood the 'alternative policies' to be prices and incomes controls plus fiscal activism, they were policies that had already been discredited.

Admittedly, the monetary side of the MTFS had a somewhat chequered record, and was ultimately abandoned.[9] Happily, however, the Conservative government persevered with the fiscal component of the MTFS, with a balanced budget being the objective in its final decade. Apart from Norway – an oil-rich country with a small population – the UK was the only advanced nation to have a lower ratio of public debt to gross domestic product at the end of the 18 years to 1997.

Moreover, fiscal rectitude was not accompanied by ever-deteriorating demand and employment. Employment was one and a half million higher in 1997 than in 1979, and gains in productivity and living standards were good by historical levels. Further, by 1997 inflation had been defeated, and prices and incomes controls had not been used at all.

This primacy of monetary policy was recognised by Blair's New Labour government from 1997. It gave the Bank of England operational independence to set interest rates and to meet an inflation target, which – at least for a time – consolidated the Conservatives' progress on inflation.

Whatever else is to be said about the episode, the intensity of the debate over the 1981 Budget evidenced the major policy shift that had occurred in the preceding decade. In the 1960s and early 1970s Keynesianism had lost its moorings in Keynes' original work, and had moved too far left in its enthusiasm for planning, including direct government interference in wage- and price-setting, and its fiscal adventurism. Monetarism proved to be a better approach – however much most British economists are reluctant to admit it. Similarly, the excellent macroeconomic results in the Great Moderation from 1992 to 2007, with its 'NICE' years of Non-Inflationary Consistent Expansion, can be explained by fiscal probity and steady growth of the quantity of money at much lower rates than in the 20 years before 1992. The once fashionable panaceas of the university Keynesians – prices and incomes policies, and fiscal stimulus and fine-tuning – had nothing to do with it.

Unfinished business?

I was fortunate to be involved with the Centre for Policy Studies almost from the start. The debates about economic policy in those years were occasionally too bitter, but they were exciting and important. So much was at stake.

I will always be grateful to Keith Joseph and Margaret Thatcher for creating the Centre at a crucial moment in British economic policy-making, and to Alfred Sherman for inviting me – as a young man – to play a role in the evolution of high-level thinking about macroeconomics.

Although my later role in actual policymaking was marginal, my commentary and writing did have an impact on decisions through the

1980s and 1990s, during my time as a member of the Treasury Panel, for example. This impact was undoubtedly enhanced by the scope to use the Centre as an outlet for monetarist ideas and proposals.

The Centre for Policy Studies may not (yet) have restored a classically liberal Britain, and industrial policy, price controls and protectionism might be in vogue once more. But the success of its work is one reason that hardly anyone nowadays considers the future to be a world in which money and private property will have been banned, and where every important feature of production and income distribution will be planned by the state.

Tim Congdon is one of the world's leading monetary analysts and authors on monetarist theory. He advised the 1979–97 Conservative government on economic policy, serving as a member of the Treasury Panel from 1992 to 1997.

7 The Economics of Thatcherism: Paradigm Shift or Interlude?

RYAN BOURNE

In 2002, Margaret Thatcher spoke at a Hampshire dinner for Conor Burns, now the MP for Bournemouth West. In the question and answer session, she was asked to name her greatest achievement. The Iron Lady famously replied: 'Tony Blair and New Labour. We forced our opponents to change their minds.'[1]

Just three years later, however, Thatcher found herself speaking at a book launch for Sir Alfred Sherman, the prickly yet brilliant former Director of the Centre for Policy Studies. Her participation that night was notable, because of the title of Sherman's short but powerful account of the Thatcherite revolution: *Paradoxes of Power: Reflections on the Thatcher Interlude.*[2]

So which is it? Did Thatcher, and Thatcherism, transform Britain to the point where even its opponents accepted its core tenets? Or was it an incomplete counter-revolution – a temporary eruption of radicalism that had not only stalled, but was already being reversed by the early 2000s?

This is a question to which even those of us who self-identify as Thatcherites often struggle to come up with an answer. As political debates wax and wane, we swing from celebrating a world profoundly transformed by Thatcherism's vanquishing of state socialism, to bemoaning the absence of market-friendly politicians and policies. We talk as if Thatcherism were an enduring paradigm shift in Britain's political economy, but also imply (like Sherman) that it was a one-off advance, the spirit of which we'd love to rekindle.

Partly, this discrepancy stems from people judging Thatcherism by different standards. For some, answering the question of 'paradigm shift or interlude' starts with an assessment of specific policies. Did 1980s reforms like privatisation, disciplined macroeconomic policy, tax cuts and reforms, spending restraint, de-unionisation and the removal of microeconomic controls endure?

For others, the legacy of Thatcherism can only really be judged according to the willingness of today's political class to apply its more timeless principles. Shirley Robin Letwin reckoned that Thatcherism, while certainly not libertarian, saw free-market economics and a restrained state as crucial in inculcating 'vigorous virtues' among the British people – the virtues of self-reliance, personal responsibility, a strong work ethic and a commitment to individual freedom.[3] Such an ideological framing allows one to judge many contemporary decisions against a Thatcherite yardstick, even on issues very different from those which preoccupied the Thatcher government in 1980s Britain.

Thatcher herself, as other contributors to this volume have made clear, definitely saw her agenda as guided by certain ideological stars. Her memoirs (like Nigel Lawson's) talk of an unfinished project.

Given the very different economic challenges today – deglobalisation, a rapidly ageing population and slow productivity growth – it makes little sense to judge Thatcherism's legacy by the standard of whether a given prime minister is an effective karaoke act for her specific policies of 40 years ago.

But it's also depressingly obvious that the broader conception of Thatcherism as an ideology or a set of values has little purchase among Tory MPs today. Though much of the party's membership remains animated by those principles and Cabinet ministers will line up to pay homage to Thatcher's big picture achievements, most Conservative politicians are what I would call 'I'm a free marketeer but…' conservatives. Everything after the 'but' implies that they do not share, or else never truly understood, Thatcher's arguments for why market-grounded economics was such an important part of her agenda.

Thatcher's economic policy legacy
It is easy to think of a host of Thatcherite policies that have mostly stood the test of time and imply that Thatcherism was a transformative paradigm shift. Exchange controls never returned. Capital still remains mobile. Even a hefty bout of inflation recently didn't lead to the re-adoption of 1970s-style price and wage controls (with the partial exception of the energy sector).

The sort of hydraulic Keynesianism that said you could trade off unemployment and inflation by manipulating the budget deficit? That was buried in the 1980s and has not returned. Despite a brief flirtation with fiscal activism after the Great Recession, most elite debates still consider monetary policy the front line for 'managing' the business cycle. In spite of deviations under Boris Johnson and Liz Truss, the Conservative Party therefore generally continues to prioritise fiscal responsibility and the reduction of budget deficits as key objectives, albeit while borrowing substantial sums whenever crises hit, before having to course-correct.

The trade union reforms also endure, as do generally quite liberalised product and labour markets, despite the evident possibility of Keir Starmer's Labour beefing up labour market regulation, making us more like other European countries. Yes, Brexit has introduced new trade barriers with Europe. However, both major political parties still profess their commitment to the ultimate goal of Britain as a free-trading nation, albeit with a bubbling fervour of support for various industrial policies, 'Buying British' and national security exceptions to open markets.

Beyond these undoubted major achievements, however, it is undeniable that Thatcherism's policy legacy has been diluted. Actively targeting the money supply as a means of restraining inflation proved extremely difficult in practice and was (as Tim Congdon writes elsewhere) abandoned by Thatcher's government in the mid-1980s. More alarmingly, the essential insight that inflation, to cite Milton Friedman, 'is always and everywhere a monetary phenomenon in the sense that it is and can be produced only by a more rapid increase in the quantity of money than in output' appears to have been utterly forgotten. During the pandemic, the independent Bank of England simply paid no heed to what was happening to the broad money supply. The result was double-digit inflation, for the first time since 1982.

Similarly, as Sherman himself documented, the *process* of privatisation initially went well. By 1998, a presentation at an OECD plenary – and indeed a major programme of research commissioned by the CPS – found that labour productivity had grown at faster rates in the privatised industries. Real prices had fallen in gas and telecoms, the water sector had seen much-needed investment and levels of service quality had risen as a result.[4]

Yet since then the backsliding has started and disappointment has set in. The inherent problems of a franchising model, which tried to artificially create competition by separating track and train operations, are leading to a gradual re-nationalisation of the railways. The anti-carbon agenda, coupled with higher wholesale energy costs, has led to a complete mess of government intervention in energy, which has even seen price controls. We might not have gone the whole hog of re-nationalisation, but we have certainly seen much re-governmentalisation.

Much of the debate over Thatcherism's legacy obviously centres on the burden of taxation. Today, it exceeds any level seen since the 1970s and is set to rise to its highest level since the Second World War. A sharp cry from the swashbuckling, tax-cutting agenda of the 1980s, right?

Well, not quite. The Thatcher government actually raised taxes pretty dramatically at the start of the 1980s as part of its macro-economic efforts to quell inflation. It was only by the very end of Thatcher's premiership that the tax burden was falling sharply relative to that she inherited, after a decade of robust productivity growth and spending restraint.

At least part of that improvement in productivity growth occurred, of course, because Thatcher's governments *reformed* taxes. Her Chancellors were not always consistent, but they generally sought to rationalise and simplify the code towards indirect taxation and broad-based taxes, with low marginal rates. By contrast, since 2010, the personal income tax allowance has been made more generous and then more stingy, corporation tax has been cut then raised, stamp duties have been suspended for 'holidays', while VAT has been raised and then the base eaten into due to the campaigns of various lobby groups. The founding and subsequent abolition of the Office for Tax Simplification within just 13 years exemplifies the lack of a coherent approach.

Ultimately, however, the tax burden will be dictated by spending. And it's here that Thatcher's agenda has witnessed its most significant retreat.

Under her premiership, total managed expenditure fell from around 40% of GDP to 35%. Today, the Conservatives preside over a state that accounts for around 44% of GDP, up from the 40% seen pre-financial crisis. And again, this is set to rise hugely.

It is true that there has been a once-in-a-century pandemic and several other crises in the interim, as well as growing spending pressures associated with an ageing population. But there has been little effort to mitigate or reduce this ratchet. Even David Cameron and George Osborne's deficit reduction programme proved to be a slow-moving fiscal patch-up job, rather than a root-and-branch rethinking of the contours of government. It should be obvious now that piecemeal 'deficit reduction was not enough', to echo Keith Joseph's warning about the limits of monetarism. And having spent most of the 2010s blaming all ills on 'austerity', a future Labour government will surely increase spending and the tax burden further.

The decline of Thatcherism

What then of Thatcherism, the ideology? Certainly, Conservative politicians still like to wrap themselves in the label. The entire leadership debate between Liz Truss and Rishi Sunak in 2022 was predicated on whether it was more Thatcherite to cut taxes or reduce deficits by raising them.

But beyond these attempts to claim the legitimating mantle, there is little evidence that the Conservative Party is still Thatcherised in terms of its thinking. In that respect, Thatcher didn't achieve quite what Clement Attlee managed for Labour – a permanent shift in how people viewed the roles and responsibilities of the state.

For most of the past decade, for example, the Conservative Party failed to identify lagging economic growth as the country's biggest challenge, let alone to develop a market-led supply-side agenda worthy of that challenge. It's not as if they were not warned that deficit reduction alone was no route to strengthening growth. Andrew Tyrie, then Chair of the Treasury Select Committee, published an important CPS pamphlet, back in 2011, making just this argument about the need for a new supply-side agenda.[5] By the mid-2010s it became blindingly obvious that a 'catch-up' of productivity growth wasn't coming and that Britain was in the grips of relative stagnation.

We can debate what caused this downturn, but an attempt to reverse it necessarily required rethinking some growth-sapping economic policies developed in what Tyrie called 'the age of abundance' of the 2000s. Yet with the deficit reduction programme and then Brexit, political capital was expended elsewhere.

To the extent growth was discussed, it was often cited as a secondary benefit of various political objectives (such as 'green growth' and 'regional rebalancing'), despite the fact that many of these policies will probably do more to inhibit growth than promote it.

The result is that while we've had attempts to reform this or that regulation, there has not been a sustained effort to raise our growth potential by making the supply side of the economy more efficient. So despite the CPS's frequent warnings on the topic, we are left with a tax system that is an incoherent mess, planning laws that are anti-development, a dysfunctional energy market, damaging regulation seen as sacrosanct and a welfare state that has gone largely unreformed.

Indeed, while Thatcher's Conservatives helped roll back the state in some key areas, she failed to address many of the worst legacies of the Attlee government. The post-war planning system has become a noose that's got tighter and tighter as the country has grown, with development in successful areas subject to all kinds of artificial restraint. Remarkably, a large proportion of Conservative MPs now urge us to ignore these market signals of where and how people want to live. Almost all the debate is cast, as Martin Wolf has put it, in Soviet terms of 'need', not demand, and over numbers of houses, not prices.[6] When it comes to housing, a lot of Tory MPs abandon Thatcherite principles and become reliable central planners.

Another slow-seeping poison pill from the Attlee days is age-related spending on health and the state pension. As recently highlighted by the CPS in its essay collection *Justice for the Young*, this is driving up Britain's long-term debt – and the size of the state – to historically unprecedented levels.[7]

Yes, demands for health and social care and retirement income would still exist and be growing even if greater provision came from the private sector, funded by personal saving. Yet the Conservatives have made the fiscal numbers worse through the triple lock on the state pension, and by chucking more and more money at an unreformed NHS. They've broadly accepted a policy of 'socialising the cost disease', as one American analyst puts it, rather than encouraging greater public and private supply through removing output-constraining regulations. The result is less pressure to innovate, leading to the toxic combination of both high spending and unsatisfactory services.

There are many more examples of this. When the Government came up with its plan for social care, it did not urge greater personal responsibility, or attempt to set up an insurance market backed by housing wealth. It simply decided to pour in more cash – in other words, subsidising the inheritors. Indeed, many modern Conservatives appear to believe that whenever there is a problem in the economy, the Government should step in.

Childcare, for example, is becoming more expensive as wages rise, parents demand more intensive learning environments and regulations implemented in the name of 'improving quality' restrict the supply of care. The Conservatives recently sought to relax some staffing regulations to offset this – a worthy supply-side reform. Yet the quid pro quo they offered for doing so was to ramp up the governmentalisation of the sector by extending 30 hours of 'free' childcare to one- and two-year-olds. An incoming Labour government will almost certainly universalise this for all children younger than school age, completing a virtual takeover of a sector that until very recently was the domain of parents and families.

One really could go on and on in this vein. Today's Conservatives seem intent not on freeing individuals and companies to produce wealth, but on 'global leadership' in regulating things, whether Big Tech or our lifestyles. Many of the party's MPs get really excited about trying to revive high streets, despite the fact the public vote with their wallets against them. Meanwhile, the Tories have acquiesced as social, environmental and health and safety regulations have replaced price and output controls in bogging down our economy through compliance bureaucracies. Bar some of Jeremy Hunt's efforts on finance, there appears to be little sustained effort to reassess the swathe of inherited EU regulation. Indeed, 'deregulation' has almost become a dirty word again. Just look at the issues that are animating the Government in its probable final year: banning disposable vapes, introducing new regulators for football and digital markets, preventing landlords and tenants from agreeing fixed-term tenancies, and, more recently, even a proposal that those putting their properties on AirBnB must obtain formal planning permission.

Left-wing commentators love to trot out lines about 'the same old Tories'. But this isn't Margaret Thatcher's Conservative Party. It is not animated by economics in the same way. It does not start from the premise of seeing private solutions as more powerful and enduring in alleviating social and economic problems. It sees 'on your bike'-style calls for personal responsibility as an insult, promising instead that governments can move the mountain to Mohammed by bringing good jobs and investment to every town and city, while protecting us all from our own choices.

One can go through all the ideals we associate with Thatcherism – private property rights, light-touch regulation, spending restraint, individual responsibility and so on – and find policy after policy where the modern Conservatives have departed fundamentally from those principles. Sherman's contention that Thatcherism was merely an interlude looks more and more correct.

From the sick man of Europe to… a sick-ish man again

'Compare our position today with that of our neighbours in north-west Europe – Germany, Sweden, Holland, France. They are no more talented than we are. Yet, compared with them, we have the longest working hours, the lowest pay, and the lowest productivity per head. We have the highest taxes and the lowest investment.'[8]

That was Keith Joseph, speaking in Upminster in June 1974. And in the big picture, the measures that he and Margaret Thatcher brought in –

Thatcherism 1.0 – worked as they hoped. Britain was the 'sick man of Europe' by the 1970s, with dismal productivity, dysfunctional nationalised industries and poor labour relations. Yet economic growth was much faster than other competitor countries through the 1980s and 1990s, leading to a catch-up in real GDP per capita that was genuine and meaningful.

From 1980 through 2011, the UK saw a stronger productivity performance than France, Germany and even the US. A lot of that was owed, as the economist John Van Reenen has said, to the medicine that Thatcherism delivered: product and market competition, the withdrawal of industrial subsidies, privatisation and more flexible labour markets.

Since the 2007 financial crisis, however, the UK's real growth performance has been underwhelming. Among the G7 countries, only Italy has experienced worse average wage growth. We find ourselves once more in a situation where we work longer hours than those European neighbours, have the lowest level of investment as a share of GDP, a high and rising tax burden, and most damningly, almost the lowest GDP per capita after a comparatively abysmal growth performance. Britain has not just squandered the chance to differentiate itself by getting closer to the fast-growth American model; we've regressed.

True, things aren't quite as bad as they were when Keith Joseph delivered the speech above, which Sherman crafted. Unemployment has stayed remarkably low, a testament to Britain's still liberal labour markets. Jeremy Hunt, the Chancellor, is right that the country has a host of other strengths – including some remarkable cutting-edge research facilities, top universities and a world-leading financial sector. Liz Truss, if nothing else, has now managed to get both major parties to agree that a lack of growth is the country's biggest challenge. The current Government is doing some things on tax and planning that will improve growth prospects, at the margin.

However, it's hard to overlook that the last 15 years represent another period of relative decline. You can feel it in the quality of public services, the poverty of ambition of both parties' leaders, the struggles of many families, and the gradual ratcheting up of spending, regulation and taxation.

While the answer cannot be to repeat the specific policies of the 1980s, the country seems to be crying out for a similarly fresh, powerful agenda for economic revival.

Looking on from my new home in Washington, DC, the Conservative Party right now seems incapable of that task. After five prime ministers in 13 years, it's not clear what it stands for. There are factions within the party, of a national conservative bent, who advocate for downplaying economic issues in favour of focusing on flag and community. There is still a large group of technocratic centrists, who'd prefer the Conservatives to represent a continuation of New Labour. And even many MPs who align themselves with Thatcherite principles rhetorically seem to believe that simply applying the same strategies as in the good old days will suffice.

On top of this, the broader intellectual environment is hostile. Economists in academia are becoming more politicised in a collectivist direction. Despite the Guardianista belief that the world is run from Tufton Street, the resources and budgets available to the technocratic centrist and left-wing think tanks vastly exceed those available on the centre-right. Add to this the general hostility towards free-market economics in the media and Whitehall and the realignment of politics along cultural lines, and navigating a path to any sort of free-market economic agenda is extremely difficult.

The unenviable but crucial role of the Centre for Policy Studies, then, is to keep alive the broader Thatcherite ideals – and to apply those principles to create a policy agenda equal to the very different challenges we face today. That means research and advocacy on the major economic afflictions that we face, including lagging growth, flagging public sector productivity, ongoing housing dysfunction and the regulation of emerging technologies. But it also requires thinking through Britain's place in the world post-Brexit, understanding the barriers and vested interests that will resist such reforms, and realising the limits of pure economics in dealing with deeper-rooted cultural and social problems.

Sherman's book reminds us that the CPS was originally founded with the aim of 'thinking the unthinkable, questioning the unquestioned'. As he concluded, 'we generated considerable momentum' in the 1980s. Today, the CPS is well placed to lead the next great campaign against British decline. My goodness, the country needs it.

Ryan Bourne is the R. Evan Scharf Chair for the Public Understanding of Economics at the Cato Institute and a weekly columnist for The Times. He is the editor of The War on Prices: How Popular Misconceptions about Inflation, Prices, and Value Create Bad Policy.

8 Back to the 1970s?

NIALL FERGUSON

This essay was originally delivered as the Keith Joseph Memorial Lecture in November 2023.

What I am going to say tonight will not make me very popular. So let me apologise at the outset to my friends in the current Government.

I saw many of them at Hampton Court on Monday at the Global Investment Summit, and listened with interest as they made the case for investing in Britain to an audience of foreign investors. They did a good job – a very good job. And I am not here to disagree with anything that was said on Monday about Britain as a destination for international capital. Still, I did find myself looking at my shoes on more than one occasion – and remembering how those feet felt five decades ago.

The soaring price of school shoes gave me my start in economics. My first-ever publication was a letter on that subject to the Glasgow Herald in 1974, when I was 10 years old.

Retail price inflation in the UK ultimately exceeded 25% in late 1975. Britain's experience was not the worst in the OECD – Portugal and Spain were worse – but it was pretty bad.

The roots of the inflation were partly monetary. The annual broad money growth rate exceeded 20% in 1972 and 1973. The Bank of England hiked rates in 1972 and 1973, but victory was declared prematurely and rates were cut in 1974, 1975–6 and 1977.

The roots of the inflation were also partly fiscal, with a succession of government deficits in excess of 4% of GDP.

Growth was also slower than in peer countries. It averaged below 2%, worse than most of the big European economies.

For investors, the 1970s were the worst decade since the 1910s, with negative real returns on both equities and bonds. Real returns on stocks were terrible. Adjusted for inflation, the FT All-Share Index from 1974–9 sat at less than half its 1972 peak. And there was a housing bubble and bust.

What made the 1970s in the UK so much worse than in most developed economies?

I am afraid part of the blame lies with a Conservative government. With Ted Heath at the helm from 1970 to 1974, there was excessive fiscal stimulus, which led to the short-lived 'Barber Boom'. There was too-loose monetary policy: Competition and Credit Control by the Bank of England; the lifting of ceilings on bank advances; the break-up of the high street banks' cartel; a new reserve asset ratio rule. There was the relaxation of controls on property development and the abolition of the Land Commission, which Labour had established in 1967 with the seemingly contradictory goals of supplying land for development and imposing a 'betterment levy'.

The bust that followed the boom was a rather familiar kind of financial crisis as novel financial institutions – SCOOP, London and County Securities, Cedar Holdings, Triumph Investment Trust – had to be rescued. The Bank of England had to buy five firms, including Slater Walker Ltd., and bail out the Crown Agents.

The Labour government elected in 1974 and led by Jim Callaghan after 1976 therefore inherited a considerable mess. It is often forgotten that the first effort to impose monetary discipline was by Callaghan's Chancellor, Denis Healey. But, as Keith Joseph pointed out, monetarism was not enough.

All this explains why 'Crisis, What Crisis?' was such a terrible headline for the Labour government in early 1979 – though what Jim

Callaghan actually said was: 'I don't think that other people in the world would share the view [that] there is mounting chaos.'

The reason those words rang hollow was that middle-class families were being hit painfully hard from all directions. 'You can't realize how near we are to catastrophe,' the historian AJP Taylor wrote to his wife in July 1974. 'Many serious judges think that all our banks may close their doors in a few months' time. Prices have doubled within the year and are going up faster than ever. My income does not go up. Indeed, it gradually goes down.'

Always a radical, never a conservative, Taylor was my hero when I discovered history. It rather shocked me to discover how much the 1970s had impoverished him. For him and many like him, it was one of the great mass muggings by reality of the modern age.

Keith Joseph's 1976 lecture 'Monetarism is Not Enough' was a paradigm-shifting response to this very real crisis. In part, the lecture was a clever (and I think correct) critique of Milton Friedman's dictum that inflation is always and everywhere monetary in origin.

'I have dealt with inflation, so far, as a monetary phenomenon,' declared Joseph. 'It is other things besides.' The distinction Joseph drew was 'between those economists who believe that monetary policies should be used to tackle monetary problems on the one hand and those on the other hand who believe that monetary policies can master non-monetary problems – such as union obstruction, lack of skills, overmanning, housing rigidity, lack of confidence – and non-monetary policies – like control of wages, prices and dividends – can master the monetary problem of inflation.'

For Joseph, 'monetary control' was just a starting point. It was 'a pre-essential for everything else we need and want to do; an opportunity to tackle the real problems – labour shortage in one place, unemployment in another; exaggerated expectations; inefficiencies, frictions and distortions; hard-core unemployment; the hundreds of thousands who need training or retraining or persuading to move.'

'Monetarism is Not Enough' was also a critique of government fiscal policy. 'Nearly two thirds of our national activity flows in some way from the government,' lamented Joseph. In a footnote he noted that total public sector expenditure in 1974 amounted to 56% of GDP. (This was actually a miscalculation; more on that later.) 'Whereas cuts in public expenditure rarely eventuate,' he complained, 'squeezes on the private sector are "for real". The interest rate is increased, bank lending is contracted, taxes are raised, other old-fashioned deflationary measures are used. The private sector is punished for the state sector's profligacy.' His recommendation was 'cuts in state spending' and 'detaxing and the restoration of bold incentives and encouragements to business and industry'.

But Joseph's lecture was a critique of big government more generally. He denounced 'our socialist anti-enterprise climate: indifference, ignorance and distaste on the part of politicians, civil servants and communicators for the processes of wealth-creation and entrepreneurship; high taxation; very high marginal rates of taxation; perhaps most important of all – increasing capital taxation on the makers of wealth – whether self-employed, small, medium or large… By taxation, by inflation, by the remorseless flood of regulations and legislation, by controls and by the constant and arbitrary interventions of authority, successive governments since the War have cumulatively taken away both the pleasure and the rewards that once made risk-taking worthwhile.'

'In order to deal with the state bureaucracy,' Joseph went on, 'the man-made environment of licences and permits, planning permissions and regulations, grants and write-offs, premiums and taxes, forms and forms and forms, business has become increasingly bureaucratised.'

Labour was of course in power in 1976 and had been for two years. Yet Joseph acknowledged that the country's situation was not only Labour's fault. And – importantly for my argument tonight – he offered a historical explanation of why Conservatives had mostly gone along with the various policy errors he had described.

He condemned the post-1919 decision to return to the gold standard at the pre-war parity at a time when too-powerful trade unions made it impossible to restore competitiveness by deflationary methods. The Second World War had 'further increased the actual role of the state, but also increased belief in the efficacy, indeed the virtual omni-competence of state intervention'. And Conservatives had also been responsible for 'encouraging or at least justifying mass immigration of workers first from Commonwealth, later from non-Commonwealth Third World countries on grounds of labour shortage'.

I believe that for future historians the great puzzle of the 2020s will be this: Why did a Tory government – if the singular is appropriate when we have had five prime ministers in 13 years, three of them in the last 15 months – end up unintentionally repeating at least some of the mistakes of the past?

Let me specify what I mean. In 2022 inflation surged into double digits on the back of broad money growth that exceeded 15%. And that year was not an aberration. Since 2010, the UK has had the highest inflation of the G7 countries. If one takes the 38 OECD members, 16 have had higher inflation rates since 2010, but the eight European Union members in that group are all former Eastern Bloc economies, with the exception of Austria.

The UK government deficit, which was on a downward path between 2010 and 2019, surged to £300 billion in 2020. Relative to GDP, UK fiscal expansion was second only to that of the US in the pandemic years 2020 and 2021. Net debt is now 98% of GDP, compared with 67% in 2010. The best that can be said is that Japan and Italy are worse and the US is overtaking us.

Meanwhile, real GDP grew by an average annual rate of 0.2% between 2020 and 2022, compared to 1.3% between 2008 and 2019 and 2.7% between 1998 and 2007.

The most recent figures from the Treasury recall the dark days of the 1970s. 'Figures for 2020–21 show [public spending relative to GDP

at] the highest percentage (53.1%) in the period [since] 1999–00.'
You will remember that Keith Joseph thought the figure in 1974 was
roughly similar: 56% of GDP. In fact, using a consistent measure, it was
42%. Today it is 44.8% of GDP. In 1990, at the end of the Thatcher
era, the figure was just 30%. Moreover, according to the Office for
Budget Responsibility, 'net interest payments [rose] to 3.8% of GDP in
2022–23 – the highest since 1981–82'.

Saying that the fiscal trajectory of the United States is even worse is
not consoling. The US has the world's principal reserve and transaction
currency. A smaller proportion of the federal debt is index-linked.
Indeed, at 25% of total debt, the UK has the highest index-linked debt
burden of any G7 member, twice the Italian share. The 'shortening in
the effective maturity of the consolidated liabilities of the UK public
sector' since the financial crisis from seven to two years has increased
the UK's vulnerability to higher interest rates.

And the UK also has the largest current account deficit in the G7.
A 'growing share of UK government debt… is in the hands of foreign
private investors', up from 13% (2004) to 25%. Within the G7, only
France's share is higher. And 'private sector buyers will need to absorb an
average of 6.5% of GDP in new borrowing each year between 2023–24
and 2027–28, more than twice the post-financial-crisis average'. The
'nasty fiscal arithmetic' when your real borrowing rate exceeds your real
growth rate is not to be lightly dismissed.

The 1970s in fact had significantly smaller fiscal problems than
these. But the problems of the 2020s may pale into insignificance
alongside those of the 2070s, if the OBR's recent projections are to be
believed.

Meanwhile, taxes as a share of GDP are at a higher level than in
the 1970s. Indeed, they are on track to match their peak in 1948.
Immigration has surged, so that foreign-born workers are now 19.4%
of all workers. Real household disposable income per person has
contracted in five of the last 12 years. And the UK now relies on imports

for between 30% and 40% of its total energy supply, a level last seen in the early 1970s, even as gas and oil prices rally.

Let me put it bluntly. To a greater extent than is true of peer countries, Britain seems to be in danger of repeating the 1970s – rather like one of those meticulously produced period dramas at which the BBC used to excel.

This is very striking to a man of my generation, who has lived and worked for most of the past 20 years in the US. Not only has inflation made a comeback; not only are our public finances in a deeply concerning state. There are also larger shares of the working-age population out of employment than should be the case. Without being so funny, elements of the far left on certain university campuses recall Robert Lindsay as 'Wolfie' Smith. Immigration is on its way back to being a wedge political issue again. And strikes are once again a feature of British life. Even public attitudes have reverted to new versions of 'Oh well, mustn't grumble' and 'Typical, innit?' when things don't work or the car hits a pothole.

And this is after more than 13 years of Tory rule! What on earth will it be like when Labour gets back in, under the leadership of a man who advertises his admiration of Harold Wilson?

These are uncomfortable realities. It gives me no pleasure to spell them out. And their political implication is unpleasant, too. I fear that Brexit – undoing what was done in 1972–3, when Britain joined the European Economic Communities – will increasingly be judged a failure if its net result seems to be turning back the economic clock by 50 years.

So why, we must ask ourselves, did the Conservatives get into this economic predicament?

There are three conventional answers to this question.

1a) Brexit was not executed in the way envisioned by the proponents of a more liberalised economy – or 1b) Brexit was always bound to be much more costly than Vote Leave claimed.

2a) Covid was a terrible stroke of luck – or 2b) Covid was bungled
by incompetent ministers or public health officials (or both).

3a) The Russian invasion of Ukraine was a bolt from the blue – or
3b) the United States and its allies first failed to deter Vladimir
Putin from invading and then failed to bring the war to a swift
conclusion after he failed to take Kyiv.

All of these belong to the Harold Macmillan school of historiography.
They are 'events, dear boy, events'. Note that two out of three of these
events happened to other countries, too.

I would offer instead an explanation in the spirit of Maurice
Cowling, one of the other great sages of the Thatcherite revolution.
When I moved to Peterhouse in 1990 to take up my first teaching
post, I came much under Maurice's influence and learned a great
deal from him. And trying to answer the question – 'How did we
get here?' – sent me back to his three seminal studies of British high
politics.

Permit me to treat you to some Cowling quotes that give a flavour
of his brilliant, ironical mind. It should be noted that Maurice had a
peculiar unholy trinity that he sought in his students: the combination
of 'irony, geniality and malice'.

From *1867*:

- '... the Reform bill of 1867 [was] an incident in the history of
  party... its substantive merits as it was eventually passed were given
  prior discussion... neither in Parliament... nor in the Cabinet...
  The deployments of principle [were]... assertions of individual and
  party opinion and personal and party power in a battle – as private
  as it was public – not just to establish the best constitution but to
  decide who should establish it...'

- 'Conservative governments were not the governments of the Conservative Party, but the governments of Peel or Derby or Salisbury… knives were never so far below the surface that a victor could ignore them… statements made, or actions taken, by any participant must be scrutinized, not as expressions of belief, but in their logical place in the chronological sequence.'
- 'Between the closed world in which decisions were taken and the external pressures it reflected, the connections were so devious and diverse that no necessity can be predicated of the one in relation to the other. Between the inner political world and society at large on the one hand and between personal and policy objectives on the other, no general connection can be established…'[1]

From *The Impact of Labour*:

- 'Europe, Russia, Ireland, India and the Empire will be treated in the way politicians treated them – as incidents in the history of what was taken to be the central domestic problem… The political system consisted of 50 or 60 politicians in conscious tension with one another whose accepted authority constituted political leadership… High politics was primarily a matter of rhetoric and manoeuvre.'
- 'Without understanding the perpetual nature of these motions, one can [not]… understand the extent to which they were moved by antipathy towards their rivals. Antipathy, self-interest and mutual contempt were the strongest levers of action.'
- 'The key lies in the minds of politicians who exercised ostensible power and in the relationship they envisaged with the society they wished to rule… we posit the existence of a network of plebiscitary demagogues whose… chief purpose was to jostle each other as they picked their way through the limitations imposed by all these forces to a position of creative sympathy with an unknown public.'[2]

From *The Impact of Hitler*:

- 'principles are manifestations of personality more than interests or passions and… all three form the context of political conscious-ness… foreign policy became central because politicians could fit it into the political battle which had begun in the 1920s… the domestic appeasement of the Twenties was assumed in order to attack the the international appeasement of the Thirties. The result was an alliance between a class-conflict programme in the Labour Party and an international conflict programme in parts of the Liberal and Conservative parties.'

- 'Halifax [was]… the embodiment of Conservative wisdom, who decided that Hitler must be obstructed because Labour could not otherwise be resisted… [But] it was neither morally obligatory nor prudentially self-evident that Hitler should be obstructed in Eastern Europe.'

- 'As a centre coalition, the government of May 1940… [left] it uncertain whether it was a Lib–Lab trap for Conservatives or a Conservative trap in which Attlee was the victim… Through Churchill, Sinclair, Attlee and Eden… and through Butskellism… it lasted until Macmillan's retirement, establishing inflation, disestablishing the Empire and permitting a receptivity in which the central features of Labour thinking became entrenched as normal.'[3]

All of this suggests a Cowling-esque answer to my question, how did the Conservatives get into this economic predicament?

Simon Kuper's amusing book *Chums* ultimately misses the point because he has not read Cowling. The Tory leadership elite, largely focused on the complex game of high politics and ascending the greasy pole, taking it in turns to be Prime Minister, forgot that inflation is always and everywhere a *political* phenomenon. Brexit was pursued primarily as an instrument of party-political competition and only secondarily – if at all – as a solution to Britain's economic challenges. Indeed, it was presented to voters as a free lunch, which, as a divorce, it was never likely to be.

The political elite then collectively decided that big government was needed in a public health emergency – and might even be a vote winner after the pandemic, as it had been beforehand (remember the bold spending and 'levelling up' pledges of the 2019 manifesto?).

In doing so, they set aside not only the principles of fiscal responsibility but also, in the panicked embrace of blanket lockdowns, of limited government itself, a mistake that most, though not all, democracies made. They thus unwittingly repeated the mistakes of the post-war Tories in believing the world had changed and that they, too, must move with the times.

Now, it is possible that Britain will avoid a repeat of the 1970s. I kept wanting to believe what I heard at Hampton Court on Monday. But the same foreign investors had presumably heard somewhat similar blandishments from members of the Shadow Cabinet. One characteristic feature of the 1970s was that the parties took it in turns not to deal with country's fundamental monetary, fiscal and structural problems.

If the polls are right, and if Labour does come to power next year, then we shall really have our work cut out for us.

For, as Maurice Cowling long ago observed, Labour always has represented and always will represent a genuine ideological challenge to the established social and institutional order.

They really believe in big government. They really believe in higher public spending. They really believe in raising direct taxes.

That is why keeping them out of power has been such a very difficult challenge for Conservatives for more than a century.

That is why Conservatives need – regularly – the kind of reminder that Keith Joseph provided nearly 50 years ago. No matter what your shoes may cost, my ministerial friends, you need to be kept on your toes.

Niall Ferguson, MA, D.Phil., is the Milbank Family Senior Fellow at the Hoover Institution, Stanford University, and a senior faculty fellow of the Belfer Center for Science and International Affairs at Harvard, where he served for 12 years as the Laurence A. Tisch Professor of History. He is a member of the CPS board.

9 Reinventing Conservatism, Then and Now

PAUL GOODMAN

The Centre for Policy Studies produces straightforward ideas for improving the condition of the British people. But it came into existence through a political manoeuvre.

After the Conservatives lost the general election of 1974, Sir Keith Joseph became convinced that the party needed to change – in particular, to recast its economic policy. So he refused the industry brief offered by the then Tory leader, Edward Heath, and asked for a position without portfolio, with a particular focus on the economy.

In his biography of Margaret Thatcher, Charles Moore writes that Heath was unwilling to risk Joseph leaving the Shadow Cabinet, and so granted his request. 'This was dangerous. There was an accompanying agreement that Joseph could approach Conservative donors to set up his own think tank to look at market solutions to the political and economic problems of the day. This was fatal.'[1]

Heath may have been lulled into a false sense of security by the terms that Joseph proposed for the project. 'He wanted to use the term "social market" – then an admired model from post-war Germany – in the title of his new organisation,' says Moore.

Germany's consensual partnership between government, business and the unions was then, as now, a model that the political establishment wanted to follow. 'Putting in Adam Ridley, the Deputy Director of the Conservative Research Department, as his spy on the putative board, Heath thought that all was well. He was wrong. The CPS gave Joseph the platform and back-up he needed to launch a full intellectual critique of the Heath years.' Margaret Thatcher soon joined the new think tank as its Vice-Chairman.

There is a lesson in the story of how the Centre for Policy Studies came into being – namely, that ideas, the raw stuff from which policy is drawn, and politics, the practice by which it is fashioned, are two sides of the same coin. Dreamy programmes become real through human means – which sometimes entails, democratic politics being as it is, somewhat dubious ones.

This takes us to the first of three Ps which made the Thatcher revolution happen – and which help to answer two questions on which this essay hinges. How important was the CPS (and other think tanks) to the transformation of Britain during four terms of Conservative government? And can whatever happened then be reinvented half a century later?

Parliament, Party, People

The first of those Ps is Parliament. The point should be obvious. Without a majority in Parliament, the best of ideas come to nothing – in executive terms, anyway. Programmes require legislation, budgets, Bills and resolutions. The conquest of inflation, supply-side changes, the Medium Term Financial Strategy, trade union reform, seeing off the Miners' Strike: none would have been possible without office and power.

Large-scale programmes also require a big majority. Moore's book confirms that much of what now might be called the Blob – the Civil Service, the Bank of England, the Church of England's bishops, industry chiefs, union bosses – were reflexively hostile to and sceptical of the new market-focused economics. Not until the 1983 election, which saw the first of her two landslide victories, did Thatcher's writ truly run in Whitehall.

The second P is Party. The Conservatives had a million members when Thatcher won the first of three general elections in 1979 and still had roughly the same number when she won her third in 1987. Not until 1990 – the year of the poll tax riots, new Tory divisions over policy on Europe and her ousting from office – did it begin to fall steeply.

A million members is a formidable megaphone for amplifying political ideas. Admittedly, the Conservative membership wasn't spread evenly throughout the country, any more than it will be today. The bulk will have been concentrated in what might be called the greater South-East. But a million people – more than 2% of the adult population at the time – is a considerable support mechanism.

The final P is People, and it takes us closer to the work of the CPS. Part of the cluster of people who made Thatcherism possible were themselves parliamentary: MPs such as Geoffrey Howe, Nigel Lawson, Norman Tebbit, John Nott, John Biffen, Nicholas Ridley and Geoffrey Pattie helped to give her the intellectual and practical backing without which Thatcherism wouldn't have happened.

That some of these, like Biffen (first), Lawson (later) and Howe (last) eventually fell out with Thatcher over economic and European policy is beside the point, which is that they were all there when she needed them most – namely, during the period of Conservative opposition, from 1974 to 1979, and the early years of her government.

During this period, between her election as Tory leader and the end of the Falklands War, she was broadly in a minority, in intellectual terms, within her own Shadow Cabinet and later the actual Cabinet, and arguably within the Conservative parliamentary party itself, whose impetus in electing her was at least as much to get Heath out as to put her in.

Socialist defectors and Tory radicalism

So far, so ordinary. One would expect a political leader to be supported by their party, both among its parliamentary representatives and more broadly among the wider membership (whose more senior members were for Heath during the leadership contest of 1975, but which came round to Thatcher's leadership during the early 1980s, at about the time she declared that 'the lady's not for turning').

What made the Thatcher period unusual, in a way that has not been repeated since, was the arrival of converts from socialism – two in Parliament, some more outside. Eight of the best-known of these lined up together in a book called *Right Turn*, edited by a Conservative MP, Patrick Cormack, who now sits in the Lords.

They were Kingsley Amis, Max Beloff, Lord Chalfont, Graham Hough, Paul Johnson, Edward Pearce, Reg Prentice and Hugh Thomas. Chalfont had been a minister in Harold Wilson's government of the mid- to late 1960s. Prentice was a more contemporary figure – a former Labour Education Secretary who came over to the Conservatives after being deselected in his Newham constituency by left-wing activists.

But there was more to Prentice's move than opportunism. What he and Chalfont had in common with the others was an inchoate sense, hardening and sharpening as the 1970s wore on, that the trade unions had grown too powerful and were helping to make Britain ungovernable. Some also blamed them for soaring inflation, which had reached 26% in 1975.

Amis was a well known novelist and a Communist in his youth, Beloff a historian and former Liberal, and Johnson a combination of historian and journalist (and a former Editor of the New Statesman, no less). These were all owls of Minerva – birds that only spread their wings, as Hegel put it, at the coming of dusk. In other words, people who changed their minds because the times themselves were changing.

Hugh Thomas brings us to the CPS itself. A member of the Labour Party until 1974 and a historian of the Spanish Civil War, Thomas was its Chairman from 1979 until 1991. So his tenure spanned the Thatcher period, and witnessed many of its most significant contributions to her agenda, not least the development of privatisation.

Yet as other contributors to this volume set out, it was another convert from socialism who made arguably the most significant contribution to Thatcherism at the time when the project needed it most.

Joseph's great speeches

The speeches collected in *Stranded on the Middle Ground? Reflections on Circumstances and Policies* (1976) and Joseph's separate lecture 'Monetarism is Not Enough' (1976) are arguably the founding documents of Thatcherism. The core of his argument in the last was that controlling the money supply would not in itself guarantee economic recovery, which, rather, was also dependent on growing the private sector and shrinking the public, in relative terms at least.

This paved the way for the Medium Term Financial Strategy, for which Lawson provided much of the thinking, and which Geoffrey Howe as Chancellor delivered during the early Thatcher years.

Lawson summed it up later, having succeeded Howe at the Treasury, in his Mais Lecture of 1984. In it, he set out his view of monetary and fiscal policy:

'The proper role of each is precisely the opposite of that assigned to it by the conventional post-war wisdom. It is the conquest of inflation, and not the pursuit of growth and employment, which is or should be the objective of macroeconomic policy. And it is the creation of conditions conducive to growth and employment, and not the suppression of price rises, which is or should be the objective of micro-economic policy.'[2]

It was not just on economics that Joseph's thinking set the tone for Thatcherism. Yet his speeches in turn owed a huge amount to the disputatious Alfred Sherman – another doyen of the CPS with whom Thomas eventually fell out, as did others.

While Thomas was an expert on the Spanish Civil War, he had not himself participated in it, having been a child at the time. Sherman, however, had served as a machine gunner for the anti-fascist Republicans, and maintained a willingness to fight for his beliefs. 'Sherman maintained a Marxist rigour of thought after his conversion to the right, and a Leninist capacity to identify virtually everyone else as the enemy,' writes Moore. 'His style of argument was absolute. When arguing against public spending on railways, for example… he argued that all rail track should be torn up and lines converted into bus lanes.'

It is Sherman, with his obduracy and distaste for consensus and eccentricity, who best conveys the flavour of those early Thatcher years. During the opposition years, her speeches quoted from Karl Popper, Frédéric Bastiat, John Maynard Keynes, Edmund Burke, Joseph Schumpeter, Alexis de Tocqueville, Alfred Marshall, CS Lewis, Adam Smith and Rudyard Kipling.

She may not have read these authors from cover to cover (who has?), but their eclectic range conveys something of her curiosity of disposition, character and openness to debate. It is hard to imagine any Tory leader since, with the possible exception of Iain Duncan Smith, being so open to voices outside their experience – and the Conservative tribe, at least with a big C.

By the time Liz Truss became leader of the Conservative Party in 2022, free-market economic thought had become centre-right ortho-doxy, maintained through the New Labour and Coalition years. Yet during the early period of the Thatcher leadership, this interest was seen as profoundly un-Tory, at least by the so-called 'wets', the inheritors of the Heath legacy, who still dominated the party in institutional terms.

As Charlotte Howell sets out elsewhere in this volume, the counterweight to the CPS at the time was the Conservative Research Department – then, as previously, a training ground for future Tory politicians and a nursery of ideas in its own right. These were strongly influenced by the Keynesian consensus that the party had embraced for over a quarter of a century, from opposition under Churchill during the late 1940s to government under Heath in the 1970s.

Chris Patten, then the CRD's head and later a Cabinet minister, first under Thatcher herself and then later under John Major, believed that the CPS was a 'provocation', according to Moore, and saw its hidden hand in developments he didn't like, such as John Hoskyns and Norman Strauss' 'Stepping Stones' plan, which focused on trade union reform.

This Darwinian struggle was viewed, by some at the time, as disorderly at best and illegitimate at worst – in the sense that Sherman, the contributors to *Right Turn*, the CPS, the Institute of Economic Affairs, the Adam Smith Institute and others to whom Thatcher flung open her door certainly weren't Tories (that's to say, right-wingers with an overriding attachment to the nation's institutions) and arguably not Conservatives at all.

But it is hard to imagine a Thatcher army winning through without its irregulars – meaning the think tanks in general and the CPS in particular. This leads directly to the question of whether their success is replicable today. To try to answer it, I must be a touch indirect, and return briefly to the three Ps.

The Conservative movement today

The implementation of a Conservative programme requires a parliamentary majority. Again, the point is obvious, but its implications perhaps less so. A majority requires an election, an election depends on voters – and they aren't always ready for ideas in the raw. These need to be packaged and presented.

Historians of the Thatcher period tend to divide between the idealists, who stress the continuity of her beliefs (a better word might be 'impulses'), and the pragmatists, who emphasise the hesitancy with which she sometimes pursued them – citing for example her appeasement of the National Union of Mineworkers in 1981 before her struggle with it in 1984.

It's fair to say that the longer she served in office, the more that continuity of conviction shone through. In opposition – the time in which the CPS was most influential – pragmatism, or perhaps rather caution, was marked. The history of those years sees her discovering her goals as she moved towards them, like a blind man turning instinctively to the light and warmth of the sun.

Consider, for example, how slow she was formally to abandon an incomes policy. This example is both a stimulus and a warning, or should be. The challenges of our times are different to those of hers, despite the recent similarities of higher inflation, tax and spending. The driver of many of our challenges, demographic change, wasn't a significant factor during her decade in office.

Today, the necessary adjustments to retirement and immigration, let alone public service reform, will be harder to sell to voters than may seem to be the case. The required changes to family policy are expensive and, in relation to housing, difficult for the party's electoral base to swallow. Still, the CPS has led the recent charge in making the case for change.[3]

The second P – Party – should play the same role that it did during the Thatcher days. However, the world that existed during the late 1970s and 1980s no longer does, and the same Conservative Party doesn't either. Its place as a provincially based party of farmers, business people and landowners has collapsed, along with the post-Cold War era, simplistic class politics and confidence in our political system.

The party is down today to somewhere between 150,000 and 100,000 members – it refuses to declare its membership figures, vivid evidence of its loss of status and self-confidence. This isn't a support mechanism worth speaking of. A million members would represent some 1 in 50 adults. 100,000 would be 1 in 500.

In the absence of any real social support structure for conservatism – and liberalism too (at least in the classical sense) – the think tanks will find themselves having to do double the intellectual heavy lifting. On the one hand, there are more of them on the centre-right than there were: think Policy Exchange, the Centre for Social Justice, Onward and the CPS in its present impressive form. Their product is as good as ever – and more accessible than some of those early Keith Joseph speeches. Once again, I'm thinking as I write of the CPS's work on housing, planning and ownership.

On the other hand, the way we live now is less conducive to straight-forward ideas for improving the condition of the people than was the case half a century ago. The age of spin dealt that way of doing politics a blow. Its art became at least as much about image as message, and the first sometimes got in the way of the second – a classic case being the attack, during David Cameron's years in opposition, on grammar schools, a case of the doctrine of defining oneself against one's own party going several steps too far.

If the age of spin was bad for policy, the age of post-spin has been even worse. During the Thatcher era, it was possible for backbench politicians to punt a prospective policy and see what came of it. Today, the enlarged parliamentary lobby writes up such exercises as evidence of 'splits' and 'divisions', and social media mobilises the special interests who profit from the status quo.

Enhanced scrutiny and mass participation are good things, as is a third leg of the stool, transparency. But you can have too much of a good thing. Yes, sunlight is the best disinfectant. But too much of it can kill: think of noonday heat in a desert. And ours is not a culture that easily distinguishes between secrecy and privacy.

We have not yet reached the point where prospective supporters of think tanks, like potential candidates for public office, look at the risk to reward ratio, as much for their families as themselves, and conclude that the game isn't worth the candle – in terms of risk to their safety, trolling by social media, the targeting of their homes by protestors, designation as politically active persons, and so on.

But electoral politics has increasingly shrunk to the targeting of a few hundred thousand voters in a very few target seats, with a sophisticated lobbyocracy in place to badger parliamentarians for more taxpayer funding for their particular cause. And bigger business is able to live, as its smaller competitors are not, with the attendant taxes, diversity requirements and regulation.

All this lends itself to the voter-fearful politics of the technocratic tweak, with a campaigning stress on the status quo, security and the avoidance of risk. Perhaps it was ever so – and all the new technology has done is make it more so, with AI poised to make it all the more so still.

Furthermore, the problems of the Thatcher age, in a non-globalised world, lent themselves to national solutions. You want to control the money supply? Choose a monetary target. To reform the trade unions? Pass a Parliamentary Act. Encourage exports and investment abroad? Abolish exchange controls.

Many of our present-day challenges are not so simple to address, as Rachel Wolf outlines in her essay. For example, do you want to address demographic change, which is so central to our present condition? If so, what does a policy to raise Britain's birthrate look like, and are voters really ready for such a conversation – which touches deeply on their private lives in a way that the reforms of the 1980s did not?

What next for the CPS?

During the mid-1970s, a critical mass of thinking socialists became conservatives, or at least liberals, because the times were right for them to do so – just as, on a less ideological basis, five Conservative MPs individually defected to New Labour during the mid-1990s. The time may not be right for something similar, as the state grows in the wake of war and Covid.

It may be that the work of the CPS, for the next few years, will be more like that of the Institute of Economic Affairs during the 1960s than the work Joseph, Sherman et al. undertook in the 1970s: to keep plugging away at the case for a smaller state and freer markets, in season and out of season, whatever the political climate.

But sooner or later there will be a reaction, as there was in the late 1970s and the late 1940s, against the growth of state power and reach. A sign of it happening will once again be former socialists 'crossing the floor', as a new generation comes to see that higher taxes, more debt, slow growth and socialism don't work.

Paul Goodman (Lord Goodman of Wycombe) was MP for Wycombe from 2001–10 and Editor of ConservativeHome from 2013–24.

10 Maggie, Markets and Me

DAVID WILLETTS

I can still remember my excitement when I discovered the power of the free market as a student in the late 1970s. At the time, the British economy suffered severe bouts of inflation, which successive governments tried to control using prices and incomes policies. That led to highly disruptive strikes which challenged the power of those same governments and turned economic problems into political crises. The low point came in 1976, just two years after the founding of the Centre for Policy Studies, when we went through the national humiliation of borrowing from the IMF – almost without precedent for an advanced economy. The Keynesian model seemed to be collapsing. But what was the alternative?

That was when, as a young PPE student at Oxford, I discovered two political economists who radically changed my thinking and offered a coherent account of what was going wrong with Britain. First was Friedrich Hayek, particularly his great essay 'The Use of Knowledge in Society' (1945), which showed how knowledge was dispersed and could not be centralised, which was why market economies function better than the alternatives. Second was Milton Friedman, who brilliantly analysed and demolished conventional Keynesianism in his Presidential Address to the American Economic Association, titled 'The Role of Monetary Policy' (1968).

At the same time, I was discovering the great thinkers of the Scottish Enlightenment who provided the intellectual foundations for these contemporary ideas. I opted for a course on 'Political Thought since Hobbes'. My tutor, a young don called John Gray, was writing a book on Hayek at the time. He helped me see the connections between the great tradition of John Locke, Adam Smith, David Hume and contemporary thinkers. He also introduced me to the communitarian critique of John Rawls' idea of justice: we couldn't just settle for a classical liberal idea of society resting on a social contract between rootless identity-less individuals. There were conservative insights here as well as classical liberal ones.

Sir Keith Joseph had set up the CPS to bring these sort of ideas into the political mainstream. But he wasn't just trying to influence the current generation of politicians: he also wanted to help shape politics in the future by getting these ideas out to the universities. In the 1976 collection *Stranded on the Middle Ground?* (1976), he reported that since his controversial Preston Speech of September 1974 he had spoken on the moral case for capitalism at 60 universities, addressing 25,000 students (during which he had been shouted down four times).

His argument was that Britain faced not a crisis of capitalism but a crisis of socialism. That pamphlet was based on the text of his address at the Oxford Union in December 1975, which I attended as a young student. I went to many talks by politicians, but Joseph's sticks in my mind because it was so different. No skilled glossing over of difficult issues. No banalities. No adherence to a party line. Instead, he was personally sharing with us a painful exploration of what was going wrong with the country – including the role of the Conservative government in which he had served. The veins on his temple seemed to become more and more prominent as he agonised about the answers to the questions we put to him. It was compelling.

It all persuaded me that getting economic policy right was one of the most important things that had to be done, and I sat the Civil Service exam and applied to join the Treasury. My first job was in the

Energy Division where we monitored – no, controlled – the national-ised industries. It did seem to me rather absurd that I was sitting there as a 22-year-old helping advise ministers on how much investment should be allowed.

The Energy Secretary was Tony Benn and we got caught up in battles he had with our boss, Denis Healey, about how much govern-ment should control the oil companies in the North Sea. A scribbled message from Healey was sent to me after one of their arguments asking for 'a note on the difference between Bennery and rationality'. It all made me even more sceptical of the idea of a rational, well informed and effective state. And at that time it was a very big, very intrusive state indeed. When I arrived at the Treasury we had price controls, pay controls, dividend controls, exchange controls and an extensive subsidy regime holding down food prices.

The Treasury wasn't my first introduction to political practice. I had got to know Dominic Lawson at Oxford, and his father, Nigel, asked me to work as his research assistant in the summer of 1978, after leaving Oxford and before starting my job at the Treasury. The Civil Service agreed. Nigel helped me see how free-market ideas could be turned into a political programme.

Although the free-market revolution is often presented as an ideo-logical capture of the Conservative Party, it was also a political project, serving the Conservatives' overwhelming objective of winning elections. Nigel explained to me that if people believed the only way to control inflation was pay and price controls, then Labour would always have an advantage, as they were better able to do deals with the trade unions. The Conservative Party needed to show it had an alternative which did not involve such deals: monetarism was therefore the solution to an acute political problem. (The 1978 CPS essay 'Monetarism: An Essay in Definition' by Tim Congdon, another contributor to this collection, is a great guide to this debate.)

The dawn of Thatcherism

Thomas Kuhn offers an account of the history of science as a sequence of paradigms. Old ones such as the Ptolemaic model of the solar system are propped up by ever more elaborate adjustments, until eventually a new and better paradigm takes over – in this case that of Copernicus and Newton, until it in turn becomes subordinated to Einstein's. Historians of economics, influenced by Hungarian philosopher Imre Lakatos (who built on Popper's account), talk of successive scientific research programmes. The free-market revolution was the most fruitful, effective and politically successful research programme in political economy in the post-war period.

I had become a subscriber to the Institute of Economic Affairs and remember the excitement and freshness of applying a rigorous free-market analysis to one policy area after another – all so different from what I was reading in the standard textbooks, which started with a purist picture of perfect competition and then devoted all their attention to market failures, defined as whatever didn't match the theoretical model they had started with.

The CPS was created with a more direct political purpose than the IEA – after all, it was founded by active politicians. Margaret Thatcher was there when the nameplate was screwed to the office at 8 Wilfred Street in 1974. One of the team told me he had overheard her arguing with Keith in the next room in 1975 and almost shouting: 'Well, if you won't run for the leadership, I'll just have to.'[1]

But this revolution had its origins much earlier in the post-war period. Purists might trace it back to the foundation of the Mont Pelerin Society in 1947, which led to the creation of the IEA by Antony Fisher and Ralph Harris in 1955. But British Conservatives were ahead of all that. The party gave up some of its precious paper ration in the run-up to the 1945 election so that more copies of Hayek's *The Road to Serfdom* (1944) could be printed. Margaret Thatcher fought her first election in 1950.

The role of Thatcher as an individual in this story matters hugely. Labour was the party of producers, often the male factory worker, but also of the man in power. Thatcher was outside that club. Douglas Jay's notorious quote that 'The gentleman in Whitehall really does know better what is good for the people than the people themselves' was preceded by the key contrast: 'Housewives as a whole cannot be trusted to buy the right things.'[2] Margaret Thatcher was the voice of the house-wife in the queue, and hence of the consumer. And seeing an economy as serving consumers, not producers, is the starting point for a free-market agenda.

I got to know Mrs T in the three years I worked in her Downing Street Policy Unit, between 1984 and 1986. She was very pleased that I then went to the Centre for Policy Studies as Director of Studies until 1992. At the same time, I served as Consultant Director at the Conservative Research Department, which included taking the lead in briefing her during the 1987 election campaign. She drew on the Policy Unit – brilliantly led by John Redwood and then Brian Griffiths – to come up with ideas, although she did reject many of them because they weren't politically prudent.

The CPS played a similar role – getting out in front of the debate and seeing what the objections were and what the opposition was. That helped ministers decide which issues to pursue and how. For example, in the Policy Unit I worked on the DHSS – health and social security in one department – and with my Treasury background, on issues such as the European Monetary System and the Big Bang reforms in the City. At the CPS, I could continue such thinking.

That said, Mrs T had a very pragmatic understanding of what people really cared about. I remember a conversation where I suggested we could just privatise the BBC. She just replied: 'But David, you wouldn't want all your programmes interrupted by adverts, would you?' That is a very different mentality from today's populism, which often seems focused on tax cuts above all else.

The CPS programme, 1987–92

When I arrived at the CPS in January 1987, things seemed quite fragile. The money was about to run out. As mentioned elsewhere, there had been a bust-up between Alfred Sherman, the creator, and Hugh Thomas, the Chairman. Sherman had gone and been replaced by the academic Jeremy Shearmur. It was my first experience of a pervasive problem when true believers get involved in politics – whenever things don't quite work out as they hope, they then blame politicians for a betrayal.

By 1983, Sherman and his friend and colleague John Hoskyns, who first led the No 10 Policy Unit, believed that Thatcher had betrayed the cause of true reform. Their particular grievance was that she had not radically reformed the Civil Service, which they saw as the key barrier which had to be removed.[3]

Yet Thatcher herself was wary of people who became so preoccupied with process. The story in No 10 was that she had asked Hoskyns for his advice on a tricky policy issue and he had said that she should create a taskforce. To which she replied: 'But John, you are the taskforce.' To my mind, the Policy Unit under John Redwood showed what could be done by working with the machine whenever possible – perhaps one reason why they asked for me to be seconded over from the Treasury. Indeed, John's deputy was Nick Owen, another civil servant.

The job of the Policy Unit and indeed of us at the CPS was not just to analyse problems nor to blame officials but to come up with policy proposals for actually doing things. But what were those things?

Following the landslide victory of 1983, the Thatcher government had radically shifted its thinking on the nationalised industries. Initially the idea had been to liberate them to borrow on the commercial market and then use that borrowing to impose real commercial discipline. But we found there was no neat hybrid solution like that – borrowing by public bodies counted towards total public borrowing.

So instead, led by John Redwood in No 10 and key ministers such as Nigel Lawson and Nick Ridley, full-scale privatisation was coming onto the agenda, beginning with British Telecom. The CPS was at the forefront of proposing how to privatise other nationalised industries. Keith Boyfield was a key figure in all this, having led the way with 'Put Pits into Profit' (1985). We followed up with papers on electricity, railways and the Post Office, among other sectors.[4]

We weren't just making the case for privatisation, however. We were also engaging in a lively argument across government. The Treasury often thought it could maximise proceeds by selling a monopoly. Instead, our expert authors and their steering groups were tasked with working out how to break up these utilities and open them up to competition. And we thought ideally this should be done before privatisation, rather than hope for it afterwards when there would be a powerful newly privatised incumbent.

We did also want to spread personal ownership – Nigel Vinson and Philip Chappell were key here, as well as outside authors such as Nicholas Goodison and David Howell. This linked our privatisation work with our aim of spreading direct personal pension investment, for example in Chappell's 'Pensions and Privilege: How to end the scandal, simplify taxes and widen ownership' (1988).

This was all part of a wider programme of liberalising the British labour market, capital market and product markets. We saw that combination as essential for meeting the challenge of raising the growth rate of a mature Western economy. And the agenda was so wide-ranging that many of the reforms cut across conventional Tory views and interests. Reforming shop opening hours meant taking on a powerful alliance of religious groups and trade unions. The Big Bang was not welcomed by the City establishment. Apprenticeships were trapping people in ageing, declining industrial sectors and making it hard to get them to think of applying their skills elsewhere – but they have always had an emotional appeal. Pensioners often voted Tory, yet their state pension was cut in real terms and then linked just to prices. Indeed, part of the credibility of the Thatcherite programme came from Thatcher's willingness not just to take on Labour vested interests but Tory vested interests, too.

We also developed a version of market reforms for public services. I had first proposed an internal market in the NHS while working for Margaret Thatcher at No 10, and she looked to the CPS to carry on this work. Indeed, after the 1987 election, NHS reform became a key priority. John Peet's insightful essay 'Healthy Competition: How to Improve the NHS' (1987) was part of this.[5] And of course education remained a high priority. The excellent Dr Sheila Lawlor came in as my deputy to lead this work. It included valuable contributions from her husband Dr John Marenbon, such as 'English Our English – The New Orthodoxy Examined' (1987).[6]

The CPS and foreign affairs

As the profile of the CPS rose, we had more international visitors. A senior group of policy advisers from China visited. They described an agenda which I said sounded a lot like capitalism. They smiled and said: 'We call it the Chinese road to socialism.' As they left our modest offices in Wilfred Street, they said they hoped that next time they came, they could visit our headquarters.

Hugh Thomas chaired the CPS during my time and his interests were particularly in foreign affairs, securing key international speakers. I especially remember a lecture given in January 1988 by Dr Zbigniew Brzezinski, 'From Eastern Europe back to Central Europe'. It sticks in my mind just like Keith Joseph's. That is because it was the first time I had heard a serious thinker argue that Soviet control over what we then thought of as Eastern Europe was about to collapse. As he said in his extraordinarily prescient remarks:

'It is not inappropriate to post the historically pregnant question of whether the year 1988 will not be about to see the new Spring of Nations in Europe, a parallel to 1848. It is not an exaggeration to affirm that there are five countries now in Eastern Europe all of which are ripe for revolutionary explosion.'[7]

Thomas was also close to those brave individuals, led by the philosopher Roger Scruton, who went into Czechoslovakia and Poland to conduct private seminars on moral and political issues in their 'secret university'.

The tricky issue which was beginning to loom in my time was the EU – or European Community as it then was. Oliver Letwin recalls in his autobiography that when he submitted a pamphlet to the CPS making the then novel case that Europe risked becoming a superstate (which became the 1989 paper 'Drift to Union'), Thomas became so incensed he wanted to bin the whole thing.[8]

For many of us at the time, the Single Market was one of the great Thatcherite projects to open up the British economy to more competition in product markets. Indeed, it might have had a bigger effect than privatisation in raising our growth rate. The late Jacques Delors, however, threatened all this by promising the unions in his notorious speech to the TUC in 1988 that the majority voting we had agreed to, so as to get the Single Market, could now be used to impose social regulations on Britain.

Thatcher was incensed, and the Bruges speech was her response. This was the moment when Euroscepticism started to go mainstream. In the end virtually none of the Delors agenda was actually imposed, but the damage was done. Some Conservatives stopped seeing the EU as a market-opening project and started seeing it as a dangerously socialist one. The CPS included people with both these views – neatly captured in 'Recommendations for the Intergovernmental Conference: Opposing Views' (1996).[9]

One lunch we had with Margaret Thatcher in December 1989 also led to a lively exchange about Germany. All the key CPS figures were there. George Urban – of Radio Free Europe and one of our main foreign policy advisers – has left a vivid account in a chapter of his memoir: *Diplomacy and Disillusion at the Court of Margaret Thatcher* (1996).[10] She was indeed very concerned about a united Germany, but George and I argued that a democratic East Germany would vote for unification, so it was wrong to try to oppose it. I continue to think that had she been more open and welcoming about what was a key victory for European freedom, then we might have reset relations with Germany and truly matched the Franco-German axis.

Thatcherism and the future of Conservatism

As well as all the substantial policy work, there was also the deeper question of the moral case for Margaret Thatcher's Conservatism. The first half of her premiership had been focused on getting the economy going. The critics attacked the economic costs. She replied with a stern Methodism, arguing that they were a regrettable necessity if we were to avoid the road to perdition. But by the mid-1980s, the economic reforms were clearly beginning to yield real benefits. Incomes were surging. I remember conversations when several of her advisers told her that our tone was now too punitive – we were allowed to celebrate success.

Meanwhile, her critics changed their argument. Now they accepted that there were economic gains, but said they were all due to a dangerous neoliberalism eroding our sense of community. Her much misinterpreted remark that 'there is no such thing as society' became the new focus of their criticism. We discussed this a lot at the CPS. I personally was increasingly influenced by the American neocons, and we formed strong links with thinkers such as Gertrude Himmelfarb, Irving Kristol and Charles Murray. I was proud for example that we published Himmelfarb's essay 'Victorian Values and Twentieth Century Condescension' (1987).[11]

Thatcher's response to the critics was set out most fully in her address to the General Assembly of the Church of Scotland in May 1988. The setting makes sense of it all. She was a devout Christian and believed that the people who were enjoying greater economic freedoms thanks to her reforms were under a clear moral obligation to their fellow man. She would often turn to Biblical parables to explain her case – from the Good Samaritan to the parable of the talents. She did not approve of the excesses of capitalism – I remember her saying to me that one of the advantages of cutting the higher rate of tax would be that business leaders would not need to get such high gross pay.

Some of her closest advisers, such as Brian Griffiths and Robin Harris, shared her strong Christian beliefs and were particularly eloquent advocates of her view of the moral community to which we all belonged. So for example we published in 1989 an essay by Harris, 'The Conservative Community: The Roots of Thatcherism and its Future'. In it, he cited Thatcher's 1985 conference speech:

> 'Government apart, the strengths of a civilised nation depend on the natural authority of the family, the school, the Church and our great institutions. It is when that authority weakens – and it has weakened – that nations turn to the power of the State.'[12]

There were other CPS pamphlets in this genre, such as 'Monetarism and Morality: An Answer to the Bishops' (1985). Ralph Harris' 'Morality and Markets – The Gospel of an Economist' (1986) brilliantly quoted the then Bishop of Liverpool (a stern critic of Thatcherism) explaining why it was sadly necessary to close churches in areas where the congregation was shrinking, and pointed out that the same market logic applied to coal mines.

But this left some important questions unanswered. Where did these choosing, competent, gratification-deferring, prudent, morally responsible adults come from? What kind of culture helped produce them? Was there anything in Schumpeter's critique of capitalism, so much more penetrating than Marx's?

Schumpeter recognised that capitalism did not mean immiseration, it meant prosperity. But that might depend on pre-capitalist moral beliefs which were eroded by the very success of capitalism. At the same time as we were agonising about these issues, there was a credit card advert at my local Tube station: 'Access takes the waiting out of wanting.' Was that the future?

It was understandable that devout Christians would rest their politics on their powerful moral beliefs. But I doubted that would work in an increasingly secular society. So how would one set out the case for Thatcherism without using literally the *deus ex machina* of religious obligation? Was there a secular version which could rest on the deep foundation of an understanding of human nature? Surely such an underpinning would follow the path of the great thinkers of the Scottish Enlightenment but reinforced with all that we had learned since.

Could game theory function as an explanation of human co-operation, especially when there are repeated interactions in an institution or a community? Would neuroscience add insights to Adam Smith's sympathy (what we would now call empathy)? Could evolutionary biology help weave these ideas together in a coherent account of a sustainable social contract?

Much of my writing about Conservatism since then is about this issue. Just as we depend on markets for our prosperity, so they depend on social consent from all of us. Civic institutions are places where frequent interaction promotes the mutual trust which helps market exchanges work more efficiently. Mutual dependence between the generations hold a society together. Modern capitalism is the best way of offering our children better opportunities than ours: it is essential we deliver that promise. These were all attempts to answer questions first set for me by Keith Joseph and Margaret Thatcher.

David Willetts (Lord Willetts) was Director of Studies at the CPS from 1987 to 1992.

11 Turning Policy into Action

TIM KNOX

One of the strange things about working at a think tank is that there is of course no such thing as a think tank, just as there is no such thing as society.[1] Yes, there are plenty of organisations which call themselves think tanks. But there is no set definition of a think tank and – thank God – no official Institute of Think Tanks or whatever, to which we all have to apply for certification. Indeed, I've always been reminded of Groucho Marx's line about not wanting to belong to any club that would have him as a member: the Centre for Policy Studies has always cherished its freedom to originate, investigate and promote policies based on its principles, however unfashionable or fashionable they might be at the time.

Think tanks are also very different beasts – some are more focused on fighting the battle of ideas (the Institute of Economic Affairs comes to mind), while at the other end of the spectrum lie organisations focused on a particular subject area – the Institute for Fiscal Studies, say. Others, such as the TaxPayers' Alliance, might be campaigning organisations. And we all have very different founding principles and very different aims.

As Stephen Parkinson outlines elsewhere in this collection, the CPS is in my blood. My father, Oliver, ran its publications department in the 1980s. As Editor and then Director, I oversaw more than 400 publications over the years, including works by practically every Tory leader from Thatcher through to Sunak.

One great benefit enjoyed by the Centre for Policy Studies was its heritage. All of us in the think tank world are familiar with that look of bewilderment on the face of a casual interrogator who, in answer to their question 'What do you do?', has been given the answer: 'I work at a think tank.'

But at the CPS we enjoy a unique advantage: absolute clarity of purpose. So we can tell that casual interrogator that our think tank was set up by Mrs Thatcher and Sir Keith Joseph to revitalise Conservative thinking, at a time when such an initiative was sorely needed.[2] And the casual interrogator instantly knows who we are, what we stand for, how our ideas have changed Britain. Whether they approve of us or not, they can place our political beliefs and principles. And nowadays, perhaps more than ever before, they will transmit an unsaid – or sometimes clearly expressed – feeling that: 'I didn't agree with everything she did, but at least you knew where you were with Mrs T. Not something you can say about today's bunch.'

So clarity of purpose, yes. But what do we do with it? This can be a difficult question for, as with all think tanks, we have no short-term metrics to enable us to measure success. We have plenty of proxies, of course: we all measure our impact in the media, or the strength of our reputations with politicians, or the success of our fundraising and our membership drives, or retweets and clicks.

But to repeat, these are just proxies. For us at the CPS, what really matters are not these proxies but getting our policies adopted, enacted and above all implemented. That was true of my time there and remains true today. This was after all why we were set up: to translate our founding principles – the belief in free markets, a small state, low tax, national independence, self-determination and personal responsibility – into policy. Policy into Action.

And unless the Prime Minister has a soft spot for the CPS – as she did in our early days, of course – the path from a brilliant policy idea to full implementation can be long and tortuous, as the three following examples illustrate.

Improving literacy with synthetic phonics

First, the arcane – but vitally important – world of how best to teach children to read. The CPS has since its earliest days fought against supposedly 'modern' child-centred teaching methods. When it came to reading, this entailed encouraging children to use the context of words within a story as the means for deciphering them and guessing at their meaning and pronunciation. In contrast, we were the first to advocate a brilliantly effective method which went by the equally appalling name of 'synthetic phonics'.[3]

But synthetic phonics were a rarity in the 1990s. Low reading skills – particularly among disadvantaged households – were recognised as a national problem, not least by the incoming New Labour government. As a later government paper remarked:

'In Key Stage 2 national assessment tests in English in 1995, only 49% of pupils nationally attained at level 4 or above. Poor performance of pupils from disadvantaged and ethnic minority backgrounds was often tolerated. In 1998 there was a gap of 52% between the level 4+ results for pupils from deprived households and those for all other pupils.'[4]

Setting out to challenge this prevailing orthodoxy, CPS authors and researchers such as Dr John Marks, John McIntosh, Martin Turner and above all Tom Burkard plugged away, demonstrating why and how synthetic phonics worked. They were vilified as being old-fashioned, and accused of stifling children's natural creativity. One of our opponents even wrote that we must be wrong, as 'literacy is too important to be taught'.

But by 2006, we had won the academic argument. When the Labour government asked Professor Jim Rose to review why literacy rates were still too low, his conclusion was to adopt synthetic phonics as the main method of teaching children to read.[5] As The Daily Telegraph announced in its main leader:[6]

'Congratulations to the Centre for Policy Studies and the education campaigners Martin Turner and Tom Burkard. They first hoisted the standard of synthetic phonics – the reading technique that teaches children the alphabet first, and then to build up words from their constituent sounds – back in 1996. In those days, the educational establishment was still wedded to 'whole word' teaching, a discipline deriving from the experimental approach of the 1960s which disdained alphabetical 'rote-learning'. The National Literacy Strategy, the Government's response to mass illiteracy launched in 1998, adopted the whole word method and imposed it on every school in the land.

David Blunkett, the Education Secretary who introduced the Literacy Strategy, promised to resign in 2002 unless 80% met the expected standard of English on leaving primary school. The target has never been met, but Mr Blunkett has since moved on to higher things. Instead it is the nation's children who have suffered: between 1998 and 2005, well over a million children have failed to achieve basic standards of literacy. A quarter of a million 11-year-olds are unable to read and write properly.

Yet as Mr Burkard and the CPS reported recently, if schools had been allowed to employ the phonics method, illiteracy at age 11 might have been eradicated altogether...

We know that phonics works because it was 'trialled', under a special dispensation from the Government, in Clackmannanshire. What other advances in education might not be possible, were local innovation to be tolerated and schools made accountable to the parents they serve? The failure of the Literacy Strategy should chasten [Ruth] Kelly into abandoning it and every other central prescription her Government has imposed on schools. We'll spell it out: f-r-e-e-d-o-m.'

Crucially, we did not just win the academic argument. We had to win the political argument as well. Fortunately, despite (or perhaps because of?) all the other trials and tribulations of recent years, Nick Gibb was able during his long tenure as Schools Minister to build on the progress made under Labour, ensuring that synthetic phonics was adopted throughout schools in England. This included, from 2012, the introduction of the 'phonics screening check'. This showed that 58% of children then met the expected standards of reading – a figure which in 2023 has risen to 79%.

So what? Well, it means that today there are millions of children who would, without the great work of CPS education experts and others, be unable to read properly.[7] Many hundreds of thousands would be struggling with literacy. The impact on their employability is incalculable, particularly as we now live in an Information Age. Even more important perhaps is their ability to enjoy much of our extraordinary literary heritage.[8]

So we won a war, against the lazy consensual thinking of the day; and it was then translated into policy because of the great, if relatively unheralded, work of Nick Gibb and others – with outcomes that have transformed the lives of millions and improved the life of the country in countless ways.

Raising the income tax threshold

A second example: in 2001, Maurice Saatchi and Peter Warburton argued in a CPS paper (titled 'Poor People! Stop Paying Tax!') for increasing the income tax threshold from £4,385 to £10,000. This, they calculated, would take eight million people out of paying income tax, thereby substantially increasing the net incomes of the lower paid while also reducing their dependency on benefits.

For whatever reason, the Conservative Party chose not to adopt this as policy in either 2005 or 2010, despite Lord Saatchi himself being Chairman of the party for much of that time. Many Conservative ministers actually campaigned against the idea, on the now bizarre-sounding grounds that it was good for the low paid to pay tax.

But, again demonstrating that CPS proposals can often win support from far beyond our natural political homeland, the idea of increasing the tax threshold was adopted by the Liberal Democrats. In their 2010 manifesto, it was their top pledge. As they put it (without any acknowledgement of the CPS, you may or may not be surprised to learn):

'Under a Liberal Democrat government, you will not have to pay any income tax on the first £10,000 you earn. This will put £700 back into the pockets of millions of people on low and middle incomes and free 3.6 million more people on low incomes from having to pay any income tax at all. In this way, we will help people who are struggling to make ends meet and provide an incentive to work and save.'[9]

Following the election, our idea became a precondition of the Lib Dems joining the Conservatives in coalition. Of course, politicians hardly ever move as quickly as you would like – but it is to his great credit that the new Chancellor of the Exchequer, George Osborne, then swung fully behind the policy. Throughout his Chancellorship, his Budgets raised the income tax threshold, so that by April 2014 the £10,000 threshold was finally reached.

Sadly, because of the long gestation of the policy, the impact was not quite as dramatic as originally forecast. As the House of Commons Library reported:[10]

'Overall it was estimated that 3.4m working age individuals would have been taken out of income tax over the Parliament. The tax saving over this period was estimated to be £825 for a typical basic rate taxpayer, and £676 for a typical higher rate taxpayer, in cash terms.'

The CPS will always be greedy for more. But this is another policy with its origins in our work, which has benefited more than three million people, reducing their tax and welfare dependency while also, for those who were out of work, increasing their post-tax pay and thereby improving the incentive to get onto the jobs ladder. Even though it has been partly undone by the recent freezing of tax thresholds, it has still left millions of people better off.

Freeports

A final example of the impact the CPS can have. In 2016, an MP from the new intake got in touch to say that he had an idea that might be of interest to us, an idea which could release a spirit of entrepreneurialism where it was needed most, encourage high value-added manufacturing and lead to the creation of skilled jobs in the more deprived regions of the UK.

Eight years later, that MP is now the Prime Minister and that policy – freeports – is now being implemented in a dozen or so locations in the UK. (As in our early days, it does help with the policy implementation if the Prime Minister has a close relationship with the ideas.)

While it is too early to judge the full impact of the freeport policy – the first five were only fully approved in February 2023 – there is every reason to hope that it can achieve its stated aims: to promote regeneration and job creation in areas with high levels of deprivation and low levels of income and employment; to establish freeports as national hubs for global trade and investment; and to create hotbeds for innovation. If this comes to fruition, as all should surely wish, the Centre for

Policy Studies will again have originated a policy to the great benefit of both the least well-off and the country at large.

From policy into action?

The success of these three policies – and many others which could have been included – should be a matter of pride and inspiration to all those of us associated with the Centre for Policy Studies.[11] They show that our ideas have helped to change the lives of millions significantly for the better – in all regions of the country, for people of all levels of income, for people of all abilities.

Such proposals may take many years to move from first thought to enactment. But it is also striking how their impact has been felt far beyond our friends in the Conservative Party. After all, each of the three main parties has, in the three examples above, been responsible for helping our ideas navigate the long and tortuous path to implementation.

Yes, the CPS probably does not get as much recognition as its employees would like from the world at large. We have often had to share the credit for the enactment of a policy with countless others who may or may not have played a role: if failure is an orphan, success tends to have many parents.

So perhaps the 50th anniversary of our foundation is a rare opportunity for blowing our own trumpet. And to remember that all that we achieve is accomplished by an organisation with an annual turnover roughly comparable to the average Pizza Express.[12] But once the celebrations have died down, we should recover our natural modesty and remember the wise words of our founder's good friend, Ronald Reagan: 'You can achieve anything in politics provided you let someone else take the credit.'

Tim Knox was Editor of the Centre for Policy Studies from 1996 to 2012 and Director from 2012 to 2017.

12 Keeping the Flame Alive

STEPHEN PARKINSON

I came to the Centre for Policy Studies in 2006, the year after the Conservatives' third successive general election defeat. I was there as the 10th anniversary of their landslide loss in 1997 approached. After a decade out of power, government still felt a long way out of reach.

Belatedly, however, the party was beginning to learn the lessons of David Willetts' 1999 CPS study 'After the Landslide', which compared the Tories' recovery from the electoral routs of 1906 and 1945 and stressed the importance of changing – and showing that they had changed.[1]

Part of this process saw new think tanks springing up on the centre-right, joining the CPS and other well established organisations such as the Institute of Economic Affairs and the Adam Smith Institute. One of the new kids on the block, Policy Exchange, was closely associated with the new Tory leader, David Cameron. It was where he had made the speech first indicating that he was considering standing to be leader of the Conservative Party, and where he and like-minded Conservative MPs had met to 'talk over pizzas and beer' about modernising the party.[2]

In this, they were echoing the founders of the CPS, whom Matthew d'Ancona dubbed 'the first modernisers' in his essay marking its 25th anniversary.[3] 'My aim was to convert the Tory party,' Sir Keith Joseph explained about the organisation he founded in 1974 – a mission echoed by the woman he asked to be his Vice-Chairman: 'The objective was to effect change – change in the climate of opinion and so in the limits of the "possible".'[4]

Margaret Thatcher's support in this endeavour was practical as well as political. As Maurice Saatchi recalls elsewhere in this volume, her assistance setting up its 'very cosy' office in Wilfred Street extended to helping to wire up the electric plugs.[5] Through the Centre for Policy Studies, she rewired the Conservative Party – and, with it, Britain.

Keeper of the conservative conscience?

It was not surprising, therefore, that when the Tories found themselves in opposition again, more than 30 years later, the CPS provided a model for those who sought to emulate Mrs Thatcher and Sir Keith Joseph's efforts to shift the common ground of politics by injecting new thinking and winning the battle of ideas.

It has long been a source of pride, and of mutual benefit, that there is such a thriving array of think tanks on the centre-right in British politics – competition, after all, drives up standards. But the Centre for Policy Studies' history and constitution enable it to engage with political debate – particularly within and around the Conservative Party – in a way that others cannot (though it has always exercised this role with a proud independence and a breadth of thinking).

Part of the predicament of this era – and perhaps for any political party or movement which finds itself out of power – was how to demonstrate change while remaining true to core principles. This tension – and the CPS's role in helping to explore it – was well illustrated by a report published in my time: 'Three Cheers for Selection: How Grammar Schools Help the Poor' by Norman Blackwell, the CPS's then Chairman.

As head of the Downing Street Policy Unit under John Major, Lord Blackwell had been instrumental in the 1997 manifesto pledge to deliver 'a grammar school in every town where parents want that choice'.[6] Yet at the beginning of 2006, Cameron used a speech at a comprehensive school in Basildon to announce a firm break from that policy: 'I'd better make it absolutely clear… Under my leadership there'll be no going back to the 11-plus, no going back to grammar schools.'[7]

Lord Blackwell responded with a 28-page report setting out the evidence that selective schools deliver higher standards, help children from poorer backgrounds and are supported by the public. He highlighted data from published league tables which demonstrated the 'value added' by different types of school:

> 'Based on an expected 'value added' score of 100, the average score in comprehensives was 99.51 whereas for grammar schools it was 101.97 – the equivalent of almost two extra terms' learning. Equally remarkably, the average value added for secondary modern schools was 99.55 – slightly above the average for comprehensives, and disproving arguments that selective systems let down the less able.'[8]

He also pointed out that the proportion of state-educated children at Oxford had fallen from 60% some 40 years previously to around half at the time of writing, and that the number of younger partners of 'Magic Circle' law firms drawn from fee-paying schools had increased markedly over the previous 15 years, demonstrating a disheartening reversal in social mobility.[9]

Though his report did not mention Cameron by name, it contained a foreword by his former headmaster at Eton, Sir Eric Anderson:

> 'The 40-year experiment with comprehensive schools has fallen far short of its aims. It was meant to provide, in Harold Wilson's words, "grammar schools for all" and it was meant to lead to increased social mobility. It has done neither.

… In effect, selection by ability has been replaced by selection by neighbourhood. That is not sensible, nor is it even egalitarian. This publication suggests that we rid ourselves of an outworn dogma, and follow a practical way to make our schools as good as we can make them.'

Lord Blackwell's report added depth and data to a debate which rumbled on for more than 18 months in the early days of David Cameron's leadership. Five months after it was published, the Conservative frontbencher Graham Brady MP resigned as Shadow Minister for Europe because he could not support the party's opposition to grammar schools. He explained to the BBC:

'Faced with a choice between a frontbench position that I have loved and doing what I believe to be right for my constituents and for the many hundreds of thousands of families who are ill-served by state education in this country, there is in conscience only one option open to me.'

He added, in comments echoing Lord Blackwell's research, that 'grammar schools in selective areas are exactly the motor that does drive social mobility more effectively than comprehensive areas'.[10] His principled resignation was a factor in his election three years later as Chairman of the 1922 Committee – the voice of Conservative backbenchers – a role which has kept him conspicuously busy over the last 14 years.

The debate about grammar schools captured such attention because it was a vivid example of the 'modernisation' debate within the Conservative Party – the public jettisoning of such long-standing policy was likened to the slaughtering of a sacred cow. But it also spoke to differing conceptions of conservatism. David Cameron explained his pragmatic and paternalistic impulse: 'I want no child held back, so my priority is not selection by ability between schools but setting by ability within schools.'[11] But others worried that it represented a retreat from meritocracy, and would entrench obstacles to social mobility.

It also pitted prominent CPS alumni against one another. Brady had worked at the CPS from 1990. David Willetts, then the Shadow Education Secretary, had been Director of Studies from 1987 until his election to Parliament in 1992. Yet it has always been a strength that the CPS has been able to straddle different strands of conservatism with civility.

The team I joined in 2006 was small. The Director was Ruth Lea, the former civil servant turned ITN economics editor, who had come to the CPS from the Institute of Directors, where she had been head of its Policy Unit. It is a great pleasure now to sit alongside both her and Lord Blackwell on the Conservative benches in the House of Lords, where Norman has served since 1997 and Ruth since 2022.

The other members of staff – and the people who really kept the organisation running – were Tim Knox, then Editor of Publications and later Director (2012–17). Tim worked at the heart of the CPS for more than 20 years, editing more than 400 publications – as his father, Oliver, had done before him. As he proudly said: 'The CPS is in my blood.'[12] The Company Secretary, Jenny Nicholson, raised the money, looked after the associate members and – along with Sophie Kydd – helped to run the events.

Our lectures, symposia and research continued to make a significant impact despite the leanness of the organisation – which was often a surprise to those beyond it. More than once, I fielded confused telephone calls from our counterparts at much larger American think tanks such as the Cato Institute or the Heritage Foundation:

'Hello – can I speak to your defence analyst, please?'
'Yes, speaking.'
'And who is your head of health policy?'

'That's me, too.'

'What about your economics department?'

'Well, now…'

Freedom to think

Part of the reason this was sustainable was the brilliant array of writers and researchers who devoted their time to producing our papers and reports – and the freedom they were given to explore a range of issues within the broad parameters of the CPS's commitment to freedom, enterprise and prosperity. As the rubric inside the front cover of its publications ran at the time:

> 'The Centre for Policy Studies never expresses a corporate view in any of its publications. Contributions are chosen for their independence of thought and cogency of argument.'

Ideas were explored and expounded in an agreeable setting – over lunchtime discussions in the light and airy boardroom on the ground floor of 57 Tufton Street, and sometimes over Bloody Marys on a Friday afternoon. (Among the many things I learned during my time at the CPS was the importance of the addition of a splash of sherry in this cocktail.)

That light and airy boardroom was my office for my first few weeks at the CPS, since I arrived hobbling with a stick after a run-in with one of the 'bendy buses' sensibly consigned to history by Boris Johnson as Mayor of London. Once I was able to ditch the walking stick and make it upstairs, I enjoyed getting to know Lisl Biggs-Davison, who rented a room in the attic from which she ran the Centre for Research in Post-Communist Economies, founded in 1983 by Ljubo Sirc, Ralph Harris and Antony Fisher. We had many engaging conversations about her work supporting countries making the transition from Communism to democracy and market economies, and the life and career of her father, a strong opponent of capitulation over Suez 50 years earlier (he was one of eight MPs to resign the Tory whip in protest when British ships returned to using the Canal).[13]

Next to Lisl's room was my favourite room in the building – barely a room at all, but rather a cupboard containing copies of CPS reports and pamphlets stretching back to the 1970s. I spent many happy hours reading and sorting through them, and was delighted that we were able to digitise them during my time there, so that they can now be accessed by many more people, no matter where they are located.

Among those which particularly caught my eye 18 years ago was Hugh Thomas' 'The Case for the Round Reading Room' (June 1983). Though I knew of Lord Thomas of Swynnerton's distinction as a historian, and as Chairman of the CPS from 1979 to 1991, I was surprised that such an esoteric – though undoubtedly important – topic had formed the basis for a CPS report in the month which ushered in Mrs Thatcher's second term.

Completed in 1857, the Round Reading Room at the British Museum was the inspiration of Antonio Panizzi, Keeper of Printed Books 1837–56, and was built to a design by Sydney Smirke, modelled on the Pantheon in Rome: 140 feet in diameter, with three miles of bookcases and 25 miles of shelves, it was immediately hailed as one of the great sights of London, and became a world-famous centre of learning. Among those issued a reader's ticket by the Principal Librarian were many famous figures whose work would be quoted in CPS publications – Sir Arthur Conan Doyle, TS Eliot, FA Hayek, Rudyard Kipling, George Orwell, HG Wells and Virginia Woolf – as well as a number cited with less admiration, such as Karl Marx (who wrote some of *Das Kapital* there) and Vladimir Lenin (who snuck in under the pseudonym Jacob Richter).[14]

The British Library Act 1972 had established a new national library, institutionally separate from the British Museum, but still housed in the Round Reading Room, with its collection dispersed over a number of sites. Thomas' report for the CPS sought to oppose plans to centralise the British Library in a new building at St Pancras – and posited an alternative scheme whereby a more modest new storage facility could be connected to the Round Reading Room by tunnel. It was backed by a committee of nearly 50 eminent scholars and authors – including Hugh Trevor-Roper, Antonia Fraser, Karl Popper, Isaiah Berlin, Kingsley Amis, Iris Murdoch, Jonathan Miller and John Betjeman.

His campaign was unsuccessful – the Round Reading Room closed its doors in October 1997, and the new British Library (designed by Sir Colin St John Wilson, and now Grade I-listed) opened its doors the following month. Having been inspired by many brilliant exhibitions staged there, I cannot agree with Lord Thomas' suspicion that meeting rooms and exhibition halls were included in the new building 'to give, among other things, readers a good excuse for not reading' – and I would like to think that the British Library might eventually have won him over.[15]

But his concern for the Round Reading Room – that 'vast, brilliant, and wonderful store of learning' in which Thackeray could not sit down 'without a heart full of grateful reverence' – was not misplaced.[16] Last September marked a full decade since it was last properly open to visitors – a situation which the museum's Chairman, George Osborne, agrees is 'not acceptable'.[17]

I was captivated by this paper not just because of my passion for the arts and history – which now finds expression in my job as Minister for Arts and Heritage – but because it symbolised the way that the CPS has, over the decades, provided a platform not just for the vital business of policymaking and economic analysis, but for brilliant minds to exercise their brilliance.

Upholding the cultural and institutional foundations of British prosperity

Another CPS publication by Thomas – the text of a lecture he gave to the CPS at the 1978 Conservative Party Conference – provides a further reminder that matters historical have been prominent among the think tank's concerns since its earliest years, as well as matters political and economic.

In it, Thomas made a powerful plea for a restored pride in our past, and a renewed appreciation for the importance of the freedoms which have been the essential ingredients of British achievement down the centuries. His text – 'History, Capitalism and Freedom' – was published the following year with a foreword by Mrs Thatcher, expressing her concern 'that a whole generation has been brought up to misunderstand and denigrate our national history'.[18]

In his address, Thomas stressed the need for self-awareness and constant re-evaluation by those who seek to draw lessons from the past:

'In most politicians' knapsacks, there are a great many received notions about the past, often relating to particular incidents which caused a chord to sound in their or their families' souls a long time ago but which, strangely enough since they often cause obsessions, the persons concerned have not examined since.'[19]

He also eloquently stressed the need for rigorous scholarship to combat the beguiling comfort of simplistic ideologies:

'The attraction of Marx is that he gives some order to the past; he puts the present in a firm place, and enables those who have drunk deeply of the heady draught which he offers to feel that they can suspend their critical judgement. I fear the only real antidote to Marx is careful, sceptical and disintoxicating history, carried through with persistence and patience. There is no short cut.'[20]

His wise words seem just as timely today, although I think that Lord Thomas – one of the eminent minds behind the History Curriculum Association, founded in 1990 to campaign for a more knowledge-based approach – would have approved of the reforms brought about by Michael Gove as Education Secretary. He would doubtless also have welcomed the more recent guidance setting out how contested elements of our heritage can be kept on public display and properly contextual-ised – 'retained and explained' – so that people can engage with the past in all its nuance and complexity.[21]

And in my current role, I am constantly reminded of the challenge posed in the CPS lecture at the Conservative Party Conference at Blackpool the following year – the first of the Thatcher government. It was delivered by the novelist, poet and former Communist Party member Kingsley Amis, and entitled 'An Arts Policy?' The question mark was decisive. Amis dissected recent policy statements by Labour and the Conservatives, and argued that the best policy for the arts is to have no policy at all.

I would agree with his plea for artists to be allowed to pursue their art unencumbered by top-down initiatives:

'The arts aren't like housing or public health; they have their own momentum and rate of development, and must be allowed to pursue it unmolested by encouragement as much as by censorship.'[22]

And I certainly applaud his enthusiastic (if admittedly self-interested) call for more bookshops: 'One of the simplest ways, not of bringing art to the people but of letting the people get at art, is by way of bookshops.'[23]

It is undoubtedly a good discipline for any Conservative minister to consider whether his or her job is really necessary – but few can have been issued this existential challenge as eloquently as Amis throws down the gauntlet to me: 'Think of a Minister for the Arts with no functions at all, his title a pure honorific like Warden of the Cinque Ports, a symbolic figure to be seen only at first nights or private views.'[24]

Perhaps unsurprisingly, I would firmly disagree with this assertion, and indeed with his claim that efforts to bring art to more people must necessarily entail dumbing-down – 'The trouble with bringing art to the people is that it tends to get fatally damaged in transit' – or that 'taxpayers' money paid to the arts encourages waste and irresponsibility in those who do the spending as well as self-indulgence in the artist'.[25]

The artists who produce the plays and exhibitions behind those first nights and private views certainly need no intervention from a minister. But when they and the wider creative industries employ 2.4 million people, contribute £126 billion a year to our economy and were growing 1.5 times as quickly as the rest of the economy before the pandemic, it would be foolish for a government not to seek to nurture the conditions to boost that growth even further – just as this one is, including through our extensions to cultural tax reliefs.[26] And that is not to mention the impact they have on our health and wellbeing, on civic cohesion, on pride in place, in the projection of British talent and values overseas, and so much more.

I would have liked to have been in that audience in Blackpool in 1979. But Amis' lecture – and all of these publications I have enjoyed leafing through again in the CPS's golden anniversary year – are a reminder of the important role it has played for the last half-century: challenging Conservatives (and others) from first principles, question-ing the unquestioned and thinking the unthinkable.[27] Long may it continue to do so.

Stephen Parkinson (Lord Parkinson of Whitley Bay) was Director of Research at the Centre for Policy Studies, 2006–7, and a Research Fellow, 2019–20. He was appointed Minister for the Arts in 2021, and Minister for Arts and Heritage in 2022.

13 50 Years of Fighting for Freedom

GRAHAM BRADY

The trouble with growing up when Margaret Thatcher was Prime Minister is that you could easily fall into the trap of thinking all prime ministers are like her. The truth is that politicians of her stature may lead our country just once or twice in a century – and maybe it's only the deepest of crises which bring such titans to the fore.

I turned 12 a fortnight after the 1979 election, and 15 just before the liberation of the Falkland Islands. Active in Conservative politics as an undergraduate, I remember a friend asking me – just after I had spoken in a panel discussion – how I knew the Conservative policy on so many different things. I answered that I didn't need to – I understood the *philosophy* on which the Thatcher governments were based. Telling this story a decade ago to a former minister of the Thatcher years, he responded, 'You're right! We could finish each other's sentences.'

We hadn't reached that point by accident. Margaret Thatcher and her hugely influential ally Sir Keith Joseph had understood that the collectivist orthodoxy that had grown established over many decades could not be broken simply by assertion.

As Lord Tebbit wrote in the introduction to his appraisal of the Thatcher years, *Unfinished Business*, the Conservative Party under Thatcher sought to find 'its own balance between the Conservative love of individual liberty and its respect for the traditional structures and values of society'. In doing so, its 'various emphases upon aspects of each tradition have been founded on both pragmatic assessments and rebalancing to counter the socialist and neo-socialist assumptions about the nature of man and society which had become widely accepted as conventional wisdom even within the Conservative Party itself.'[1]

Winning the war

Given the extent to which socialist assumptions had spread, it was necessary to go back and make the case for freedom and to make it from first principles. The foundation of the Centre for Policy Studies – where I was privileged to work soon after university, and am currently privileged to serve as Deputy Chairman – was a critical part of the plan to do that, bringing together Thatcher, Joseph and another key thinker, Alfred Sherman.

In her speech to the Junior Carlton Club on 4 May 1976, Mrs Thatcher showed exactly this determination to tackle the very foundations of the enemy citadel:

'One of the most constant features of left-wing propagandists has been to claim some kind of moral superiority for socialism compared with other economic systems. Socialism, they say, represents co-operation compared with the competition which is normal under free enterprise.

They claim that in a socialist society decisions are taken in the interests of all, and they contrast this with what they describe as the selfishness and self-interest of private enterprise. Indeed, they boldly describe socialism as a system of orderly and rational planning, compared with what they call the chaos of capitalism...

Nothing is further from the truth... To believe that socialism is in some way morally superior to a free enterprise system is to

believe that it is better for an official to take a decision than it is
for an individual to take it for himself.'[2]

Many speeches given by Thatcher and Joseph in those early years were
greatly influenced by Sherman, the first Director of the CPS, who
was instrumental to their establishing the CPS in the first place. And
while they all saw that the most immediate challenge was to reverse the
economic decline that had become entrenched, there was also a clear-
sighted understanding that economic freedom and personal liberty go
hand in hand.

In 1977, Thatcher told the guests at the Iain Macleod Memorial
Lecture:

'Choice in a free society implies responsibility. There is no hard-
and-fast line between economic and other forms of personal
responsibility to self, family, firm, community, nation, God.
Morality lies in choosing between feasible alternatives. A moral
being is one who exercises his own judgment in choice, on
matters great and small, bearing in mind their moral dimension
– right and wrong.

Insofar as a citizen's right and duty to choose is taken away
by the State, the party or the union, his moral faculties – his
capacity for choice – atrophy, and he becomes a moral cripple
in the same way as we should lose the faculties of walking,
reading, seeing, if we were prevented from using them.'[3]

Nothing could be further away from the bland managerial politics that
has dominated recent decades. Here was the politics of moral purpose,
free markets being restored not just because free economies are more
prosperous but because the very exercise of choice brings a growth of
humanity and dignity.

The equivalence, even indivisibility, of economic freedom and personal liberty; the responsibility to exercise choice for the good of self, family, firm, community; the iron resolve to defend sovereignty and democracy – precisely because this was the route to preserve our freedom to exercise choice as moral beings – all of this hung together as a seamless garment.

In Thatcher's time, Conservatives knew not just what we should be doing but *why* it was the right thing to do as well. We stood firm and ultimately prevailed in the Cold War both in order to defend our own freedom and to fulfil the moral mission of freeing the peoples of Eastern and Central Europe from socialist oppression.

After the Centre's first 15 years, and still in its original home at 8 Wilfred Street, it published *Policies of Thatcherism*, an anthology of some of the most important and influential CPS pamphlets.[4] This collection showed a remarkable breadth and reach: the role of the state, wider ownership, improving educational outcomes, fixing the NHS and the privatisation of state-owned enterprises. Margaret Thatcher was still Prime Minister when she wrote the foreword:

'In the 15 years since the Centre was founded by Sir Keith Joseph and myself, it has provided inspiration for many of the policies which our Conservative Government has put into practice. A number of these policy ideas, which were often accused of being impractical when they were first put forward, are now universally accepted and are being implemented by governments across the world.'

By the 1987 election victory, and even more so when the Berlin Wall came down, it seemed obvious that the battle against socialism had been won: at home and abroad. The 'Peace Dividend' and Francis Fukuyama's 'End of History' followed. Even as 18 years of Tory government sputtered to a halt, the British people only risked taking on a

'New' Labour Party that was promising to keep to Conservative plans for tax and spending for an entire parliament. Three weeks into his time as Prime Minister, Tony Blair famously invited Lady Thatcher to tea at No 10 – but it was this key pledge not to increase taxes or borrowing that was the real homage to the lady's ideological victory.

Losing the peace

The trouble is, as Karl Marx reminded us, history repeats itself first as tragedy, then as farce. Thirteen years of Labour government did not see the overt extreme socialism that would have ensued from a Corbyn-led administration. But it did entail a massive and effective march on our public and cultural institutions.

Having joined the Centre for Policy Studies in 1990, I had by this point gone on to a career in Parliament – one of the few new faces on the Tory benches in the wake of the Blair landslide. At one point, early in that 1997 parliament, there were no fewer than five local Labour councillors on the board of my NHS Hospital Trust. This was very helpful to me in persuading the Commissioner for Public Appointments to take a close look at the appointments process – but it was being repli-cated across the whole apparatus of state and 'third sector' institutions.

Even when coalition or Conservative governments came to office, the same liberal-left mindset often dominated public appointments. Only a very strong-minded minister will dismiss the whole shortlist that is presented to them and ask officials to start again. As such, those of a more conservative disposition quickly learn not to waste their time applying when shortlisted applicants are often less-qualified people with the 'right' outlook or background. Conservative academics do not expect preferment; theirs is not a comfortable twilight as Master of an Oxbridge college.

Perhaps it's inevitable, too, that when we think that an argument has been won, we tend to stop repeating it. Why go on fighting the last war?

The truth is that in the struggle between opposing ideologies the battle is never won. Margaret Thatcher told the CDU in Hanover (1976):

'My country, like yours, has several political parties but though there may be many party labels, there are only two political philosophies, only two ways of governing a country. One is the Socialist-Marxist way in which what matters is not the people but the State; in which decisions affecting people's lives are taken for them, instead of being taken by them; in which directives replace incentives; in which the State is the master of the individual, instead of the servant.

In my country, as in some others in Western Europe, Socialism has gone too far. Each year more of the decisions are made by the State and fewer by the individual. Each year therefore the State takes more in tax and leaves less for the individual. This is Socialism in practice. If we go on like this, we shall become a pocket-money society: a society in which the fruits of our work belong mainly to the State, but where we are handed back a little each week for our personal use.'[5]

Gordon Brown's tax credits for working people blurred the boundaries between taxes and benefits in a way that started to look remarkably like the creation of the 'pocket-money society' described above. Their welcome replacement by Universal Credit under the Conservatives, and the continuing drive to help people into work and self-reliance, is an important example of how the tussle between the two political philosophies continues to play out.

Sadly though, there are too many areas of public policy and public discourse where the left has been allowed to reassert itself. Perhaps the clearest example of this was the readiness with which a Conservative government vacated the field when Covid arrived. Professor Neil Ferguson famously said of the 'innovative intervention' of lockdown coming from China: 'It's a Communist one-party state, we said. We couldn't get away with it in Europe, we thought... and then Italy did it and we realised we could.'

There have been many discussions of the rights and wrongs of lockdown in the context of the pandemic. I am more convinced than ever not only that they did more harm than good but that they may have done very little good at all, and that Sweden and Florida took a better way. For my purposes here though, I just want to use the widespread willingness to accept extreme constraints on personal autonomy and family life that were previously thought impossible in a free society as an illustration of how far the collectivist philosophy has triumphed in the years since we thought the argument had been won.

Even those who still think that extreme state intervention was justified in contending with Covid might wish to reflect on whether the Government went too far when it made it illegal to see your own children or grandchildren if you didn't already live with them. Or when the state presumed to mandate care home workers or nurses to be vaccinated if they wished to work. Even the religious beliefs of a tiny number of Christian Scientists in my constituency, running a care home for members of their own faith, were overruled by the state.

I ask the reader to look again at that Iain Macleod lecture given 46 years ago:

'Morality lies in choosing between feasible alternatives. A moral being is one who exercises his own judgment in choice, on matters great and small, bearing in mind their moral dimension – right and wrong. Insofar as a citizen's right and duty to choose is taken away by the State, the party or the union, his moral faculties – his capacity for choice – atrophy.'[6]

The consequences of lockdown are all around us. Many of the challenges faced by governments today were caused or exacerbated by that experience. Poor school attendance, a crisis in young people's mental health, vastly higher NHS waiting lists and massive levels of public debt. It may be, though, that the most serious and damaging consequence will be a further shift of the dial in a collectivist direction. People may be more willing not just to *accept* things being done to them but even to *expect* it. Furthermore, a state that got used to using the police to stop people sitting alone on park benches may be far too ready to exercise intrusive and disproportionate powers in future.

Back to first principles
The reaction to Covid may be an extreme case, but it is an important one.

As we look at the first 50 years of the Centre for Policy Studies and what has been achieved in the great battle between the two philosophies of government, there is much of which to be proud. The CPS made the case for personal pensions, wider share ownership, moving failed state-owned industries into the private sector and much more. The Centre was at the heart of a movement that understood the importance of winning minds as well as hearts. From a small office in Westminster it was possible to make a big difference.

Looking ahead to the task for the next 50 years, it is again time to go back to first principles, to make arguments that have been gathering dust for too long, to engage new generations in understanding that freedom is not just economic, that choice, democracy and individual responsibility are the foundations of our civilisation; that moral choices have *to be* choices.

Governments of all parties have been eloquent in demonstrating the limits of what the state can do. Too little has been said about empowering individuals to take responsibility for themselves, their families, firms, society.

Thirty years after Thatcher's fall, we Tories are a long way from being able to finish each other's sentences. That seamless garment that linked the defence of our democratic sovereignty to the freedom to earn a living, or run a business; and then to our personal liberty – our right to make moral choices for ourselves, our families and for society – is once again full of holes. The Centre for Policy Studies is needed now just as much as it was in 1974. The challenge is the same.

Sir Graham Brady has been the MP for Altrincham and Sale West since 1997 and is the Chairman of the 1922 Committee of backbench Conservative MPs. He is also Deputy Chairman of the CPS.

14 A Conservative Revolution? Yes, Please!

MAURICE SAATCHI

Fifty years ago, the most significant event in the recent history of the Conservative Party took place in a small office in Westminster.

Mrs Thatcher was on the floor wiring a kettle for her new Centre for Policy Studies. In fact, she wasn't wiring the kettle at all. She was rewiring Conservatism.

She and Sir Keith Joseph designed the CPS to provide the intellectual and academic foundation for what later became known as Thatcherism. 'The Centre for Policy Studies,' she said in the phrase that gives this essay collection its title, and is now emblazoned on the walls of the CPS offices, 'was where our Conservative revolution began.' It worked. Four Conservative election victories followed.

Times change. Fifty years later, the wires have been pulled out. Conservative supporters now exhibit the symptoms of what doctors call *dissociative seizures* – confusion, bewilderment, a strange sense of detachment and disillusionment.

This painful condition usually requires neurological evaluation and treatment.

Something has gone wrong with Mrs Thatcher's idea of the 'free market'. It was meant to be a 'perpetual referendum'. People would cast their vote every day, and from the competition to win their custom, better products and services would emerge.

Unfortunately, it hasn't worked out like that.

After she left office, Mrs Thatcher came to lunch. I asked her if she knew the share of the top five banks in Britain in all financial transactions – loans, mortgages, credit cards, insurance. She said she didn't. I told her it was 80%. She said: 'It's impossible.' She didn't mean that it wasn't true. She meant that it was intolerable.

Who can disagree when considering the banks, the trains, electricity, gas, water, oil or many other large global industries? Globalisation led to 'cartelisation' – the creation of global cartels in which there is a huge imbalance of power between the individual customer and the giant corporation; a sense of powerlessness and unfairness that results from a world of global corporations whose governance (and maybe taxes) are beyond public control.

Five US companies are now worth more than all the listed companies on the UK stock market put together. Perhaps Marx was right after all: 'After years of internecine warfare among capitalists, there will be fewer and fewer capitalists controlling vaster and vaster empires.'

Many Conservatives suffered dismay and disappointment as the story unfolded. These were the unfortunates who trusted most strongly in 'free markets'. They struggled to understand how free-market competition could possibly lead to a situation where the capitalist model would be discredited – not by its well rehearsed moral consequences, greed and selfishness, which are part of the model, but by its unintended economic consequences, the creation of giant cartels beyond the reach of national governments. Being too big to fail, perhaps they are also too big to care.

Is this the *Anthill Society*? For those at the top of the corporate Ferris wheel, we may look like ants. They can tread on a few of us without even noticing.

Have you ever tried calling BT? Or UK Power Networks? I have. I timed it. It takes longer to get through to BT than No 10. UK Power Networks takes longer than the UK Parliament. And here comes the best part: while you wait, you pay. The longer the queue, the bigger their profit.

Have you ever heard of the people who run these companies? The Chairman, perhaps? The CEO? Any board members? Of course not. They are invisible. Anonymous. That's part of the plan.

At least with Big Government you know who's in charge. If you want to complain, you know the name and address. *The Prime Minister. No 10 Downing Street.* But with these Big Companies you have no idea.

With Big Government, you can change the leader every now and again. But with these Big Companies, you wouldn't know where to begin.

Consider Britain's two least favourite companies, Heathrow and Gatwick airports. Who owns them? Who knows. You'll need an LSE scholarship to find out. How about P&O Ferries? It sacked 800 people one night. But its ships had somewhere to get to and sailed calmly on. Or Centrica, which trebled its profits thanks to higher gas prices.

These Big Companies have a formidable army. Well trained. Well resourced. Their collaborators are everywhere. Seasoned operatives, they are hard to spot, and easily blend into the crowd. They are skilled defenders of their status quo: outwardly normal, productive, sober and respected members of the community. To avoid suspicion, they play golf and go to the opera.

They don't send each other emails. They don't dine at Wiltons. They don't need to. These companies have identical interests. Acting independently, they all automatically do the same.

Mrs Thatcher was concerned to hear that the end-result of competition is the end of competition. She knew that capitalism without competition is exploitation.

Finance? Five banks control Wall Street.

Defence? In 1990, America had 51 'Prime Defence Contractors'. Today? Five. Satellite suppliers: from eight down to four. Tactical missile suppliers: from eight down to three.

You might have thought there is at least one market that is definitely 'free' – the stock market. That is surely where the price of a company's shares is set purely by supply and demand.

But no, the Big Companies have taken that over too. Their successful lobbying persuaded the US Securities and Exchange Commission to permit them to buy their own shares in the market. One trillion dollars in 2022.

This obviously distorts the 'free market' to the benefit of shareholders and executives. It alters the calculation of earnings per share (EPS) to help executives achieve the targets in their share option plans.

This 'free market' may be creating levels of inequality in society that no Levelling Up minister can fix.

It has also presented us with a problem to which it has no solution – our own health.

Consider the NHS, Britain's proudest achievement since the Second World War.

I saw first-hand the glow of pride in the NHS slowly darken to ambivalence – concern about the present and anxiety for the future.

The NHS now is the ultimate *Post-Truth* world – *Fake News* and *Alternative Facts*. Here are a few of them...

1	All is well.	All is not well.
2	All is not well but it's under control.	The economic model is irreparably broken.
3	The NHS is in crisis.	Crisis? What crisis?
4	Health spending is rising.	Health spending as a % of GDP is falling.

5	Health spending is up on the previous Government.	Health spending per head of population is 21% lower than the G7 average, and the second lowest in the G7 (after Italy).
6	Cancer treatment is improving. Cancer innovation is happening night and day.	Only around 5% of the UK cancer incidence are enrolled in clinical trials; the rest receive the standard treatment – poor life quality followed by death. Slowest take-up of new drugs.
7	Cancer treatment is stuck in the past. Many treatments are the same as 40 years ago – medieval, degrading, ineffective.	We all have to die sometime.
8	Medical negligence litigation is a barrier to NHS innovation. Around £2.5bn in claims is now being paid out each year.	There is no fear of litigation in the medical profession.

9	The Tory government will sell off the NHS, just like the trains, gas, electricity, etc. – giant monopolies or cartels who couldn't care less about us.	A fantasy. The Government is always 'putting patients first'.
10	Bad news for the NHS is good news for the Tories. It 'rolls the pitch' for privatisation.	The NHS is 'safe in our hands'.
11	We don't want to be like the US – credit card at the ready.	As a percentage of GDP America spends nearly twice as much on healthcare as the UK.
12	Everyone should pay, or at least rich people.	We can't have 'means testing' as we are rolled into surgery.
13	Everyone should pay more tax to preserve the NHS.	We're paying enough tax. We're not paying any more.
14	'Free means free'. That is the basic principle to save people from financial distress in their hour of need.	The rich should pay for their own treatment.

15	When things go wrong nobody is accountable.	New regulation encourages whistle-blowers. We are learning lessons from errors of omission and commission in the past.
16	Doctors say this winter crisis is worse than ever.	The NHS treats over a million patients every 36 hours. A few problems are to be expected, no blame attached.
17	Labour wears its heart on its sleeve, but will do nothing in practice.	Labour created the NHS. Labour loves the NHS.
18	Conservatives love 'our NHS' more than Labour.	Tories only say that to avoid being called 'the nasty party'.
19	The Conservatives should do more to defend their 'brand image' on the NHS.	The NHS is an issue of high salience on which Labour has a high rating. The correct Conservative strategy is to shut up.
20	It's all-out war! Labour should attack 'the nasty party' at every turn.	Labour should concentrate on its economic management credentials.

21	Royal Commissions are a waste of time and money.	The NHS Royal Commission will have the power to subpoena witnesses, and require them to speak under oath. A false statement is perjury, punishable by imprisonment.
22	HMG has a health policy. It was in our manifesto at the last general election. We don't need to invent another one.	It isn't working.
23	The NHS is a national treasure. We all love the NHS.	The NHS is past its sell-by date.
24	We are not going to pay to see the doctor. They said 'free at the point of use'.	Get real!
25	Rationing new drugs by wealth is unacceptable.	Grow up!
26	The NHS is 'rationing' operations, scans, procedures. The rich are in the front of the queue.	Money means a better car, a bigger house and, in time, a longer life.

27	Morale is at an all-time low.	They said that in 1948 when the NHS began.
28	Poor people are suffering most.	The poor 'asked for it'. They don't exercise, eat junk food, are overweight and smoke and drink too much.
29	We need massive public awareness campaigns like AIDS on obesity, alcohol, etc.	These campaigns cost taxpayers money and don't work. The money should be spent on 'the front line'.
30	We need legislation on sugar, alcohol, etc. Prevention is better than cure.	Law change is unnecessary and counter-productive. A culture change is required.
31	Oversubscribing of antibiotics creates 'false hope' and only leads to drug 'resistance'.	Science will provide.
32	It's all the fault of the ageing population.	They paid their taxes all through their working lives. They deserve 'end of life' care.
33	It's all the big pharma drug rip-off.	HMG is negotiating at pace to reduce prices of innovative drugs.

34	Doctors say the NHS 'hits new performance lows'.	The Department for Health says: 'the NHS is now carrying out record numbers of treatments, with more doctors and nurses providing safer, more personal care than ever before'.
35	Doctors are overworked and underpaid. They deserve better than constant carping and criticism.	Doctors are lazy and greedy. They will not give us a seven-day, 24/7 service unless they are paid more. Top consultants are 'profiteering'.
36	We need more cancer innovation. There will be no cure for cancer until real doctors with real patients in real hospitals can attempt an innovation.	Innovation risks doing patients harm. Patients will be experimented on like mice and their bodies thrown out into the streets.
37	Cancer survival is improving.	UK cancer survival rates for some types are lower than in Croatia, Estonia and Latvia. Cancer rates are rising, not falling.
38	We are doing worse than the EU average on cancer.	These league tables overlook 'other factors'.

39	NHS spending is 'ring-fenced'.	You need a master's degree from Harvard Business School to know what that means.
40	The internet is helping more patients know more.	Amateur detectives are dangerous. Leave it to the experts.
41	It's all a question of money.	Money is not the problem. It's 'systemic'.
42	The NHS is a giant bureaucracy. Too many cooks.	The NHS is a proven system for managing a large complex organisation.
43	Cuts in mental health are the problem.	Mental health is now to be treated in 'parity' with physical health.
44	Immigration is the problem. Doctors don't speak English. Patients don't speak English.	The NHS depends on foreign doctors, nurses and staff.
45	'Health tourism' is ripping off British taxpayers.	It is only small – under 1% of the NHS budget.
46	Immigrants are taking our hospital beds and clogging GP appointments and A&E.	HMG will solve the small boats problem.

47	Pharmacies can help relieve the burden on GPs and A&E.	Pharmacists are not properly qualified to provide safe care for patients.
48	With consent, our medical records should be shared for the benefit of scientific knowledge. Sharing data is important for national security.	Patients' data should not be shared with other Government departments, HMRC, police or the security services.
49	One million NHS patients a year is a unique national asset for science.	This kind of data 'trawling' and 'harvesting' is an intolerable invasion of privacy. Our 'data' will just be sold to the highest bidder.
50	One patient can change the world.	We want 'evidence-based' medicine, not anecdotes.
51	The NHS suffers because it is a political football.	The party war is good for the NHS. It's democracy.
52	The 'old folk' are 'bed-blockers'. That's why A&E is failing.	It's not their fault! There is no 'social care' in the community for them.
53	The NHS is a national treasure, like the crown jewels.	The NHS is a national relic, like Stonehenge.

54	We need more 'business discipline' in the NHS.	The NHS is not a business. It is a social contract. The 'buyer's and seller's market' in the NHS is the cause of all the trouble.
55	We need an 'NHS tax'. People would pay if they knew it was for the NHS.	Hypothecated taxes are dangerous because they are blind to economic cycles. The Treasury needs full control of tax revenue to manage the public finances.
56	We should copy the successful 'social insurance' models of other countries.	Cross-country comparisons are for the birds. There are too many variables.
57	Politicians should get out of the NHS.	That is childish. Ultimately, they cannot and should not escape responsibility.
58	The NHS is a bloated bureaucracy of managers and pen-pushers. More should be spent on the front line.	It's not the structure. It's the culture.

59	Love of money is the root of all evil in the NHS.	It's not the money. It's the organisation.
60	It's an unfair postcode lottery.	The NHS is working hard to level up the mediocre and failing hospitals.
61	NHS Digital has been created to advance the dissemination of scientific knowledge and diffusion of best practice.	Facebook knows what kind of lettuce we like and what we had for breakfast. But NHS Digital may sell our most intimate private details to advertisers.
62	There is too much waste in the NHS purchasing system for drugs and equipment.	Top-level accounting professionals from the private sector have been brought in to advise HMG.
63	Doctors and nurses should run the NHS.	They have no idea about money.

It's no surprise that Conservative supporters are confused and bewildered. They don't know what to think.

Reading all this, you may wonder why someone doesn't just privatise the whole thing and put it out of its misery.

One thing is certain. We are not going to pay more tax for the NHS. We're paying enough tax already. Record taxes, in fact. We are also not going to pay for NHS treatment because it is meant to be 'free at the point of use'.

We have worked out that there is a new, top-secret government policy in place. Very hush hush. It has a name. *Rationing by Waiting.* Your knee operation will still be free, it's just that you will have to wait a year. If you don't want to wait, go private.

We have grown used to 'tiered services' from airlines or streaming channels that offer a 'basic' service with extra features for £X.

The NHS has joined their club. If you don't like the delay, pay.

All this is a symptom of a wider problem – the one addressed in the first half of this essay. Being the Chief Spokesperson for the 'free market' is no longer a winner.

Big Companies think they are *Big Daddy*. To them, we are helpless administrative units with no power or influence. They commit what the Pope calls 'the modern sin. The sin of indifference.' A shrug of the shoulders. Nobel Laureate Wislawa Szymborska described them well:

'If snakes had hands, they'd claim their hands were clean.'

Perhaps it's time to rescue the ants from *Big Daddy*:

'Daddy, Daddy, you bastard, I'm through.'

Only the Conservative Party can do that. Because freedom, independence and self-determination are the core of its body. Perhaps a Royal Commission on Health will help it recover its heartbeat.

Can dissociative seizures be treated? Certainly. And hopefully it won't be another 50 years before the new Mrs Thatcher comes along.

So come on, you Conservatives!

Man the ideological barricades!

Maurice Saatchi (Lord Saatchi) was Chairman of the Centre for Policy Studies from 2010 to 2020. He is the cofounder of Saatchi & Saatchi and M&C Saatchi, and author of Do Not Resuscitate (ERIS, 2022). He is a former Governor of the London School of Economics and the author of numerous influential Centre for Policy Studies reports. He was elevated to the peerage in 1996. He served on the Conservative front bench in the House of Lords as Shadow Minister for the Treasury and the Cabinet Office between 1999 and 2003. He was Chairman of the Conservative Party from 2003 to 2005.

15 What Next?
Fixing the State

RACHEL WOLF

The first official meeting of the CPS's management committee, in May 1974, was held in the aftermath of strikes and the three-day week; IRA bombs; and Enoch Powell's 'rivers of blood' speech. The previous October, Arab armies had launched a surprise attack on Israel.

The Conservative Party was considered by many to have lost its way – unable to take strong decisions and too indistinguishable from the Labour Party. When Heath had gone to the country with the question 'who governs Britain?', the result was a hung parliament.

So far, so familiar. There was a sense, then as now, that the Government wasn't in control. Politicians pulled levers, but things got worse. There was no real belief that a different party would improve the situation.

The parallels between 1974 and 2024 have been mentioned by many contributors to this essay collection. But Britain has changed substantially over the past 50 years. Paul Goodman argues elsewhere that any programme of Thatcherite renewal would face significant structural obstacles: the decline in membership of the political parties, the leftward tilt of academia, the spin-driven nature of modern politics.

What Paul says about parties and politics is even truer of the country. There have been profound social, economic and demographic changes in the last 50 years. Any Thatcherite renewal must recognise this – and must focus beyond just the economy. In particular, it is my

187

view that we need to devote far more attention to the functioning and structure of the state.

Same values, different frustrations

Thatcher had a great genius for explaining economic ideas in moral terms: or perhaps more accurately, she was attracted to the economic ideas that matched her moral philosophy. And while the language was different – in particular, as David Willetts and Dominic Sandbrook note, it was much more informed by the shared Christian vocabulary of Britain 50 years ago – that moral philosophy still holds.

The polling evidence shows that family, fairness and freedom are our most important values.[1] People still believe that decency and hard work should be rewarded. People in Britain long to be proud of Britain. Despite a huge gulf since 1974 in many other aspects of British life, the same ideals prevail – and across class and race.

What is absent, now as then, is a belief in politicians' interest or ability to deliver.

However, there are differences. Thatcher's radical policy decisions were a necessary response to the challenges of the time. Today's radical policy decisions must be different, because the challenges are different, even if the fundamental values of the CPS, and the pervasive sense of malaise, are much the same.

So how different were things in 1974? Here are 10 obvious factors for any politician, or political thinker, to bear in mind.

1. Britain in 1974 was much smaller, with around 12 million fewer people in the country.[2] We were also losing people rather than gaining them – net migration was negative throughout the 1970s, as it had been throughout the preceding century.

2. Britain was a lot younger. Some 29% of the population were under 18 and only 14% over 65. Now the numbers are roughly equal:

22% of the 2019 population were under 18 vs 19% who were over 65. But this will soon flip: we already have three times as many over-85s as in 1974.[3]

3. Britain was overwhelmingly white and overwhelmingly British. We don't know exactly how white, because the Census didn't ask about ethnicity until 1991. But we know that even by then, 93% of people reported themselves as being white British, compared with 75% today.[4] Since ethnic minorities have a younger age profile, and net migration is very high, we should expect that trend to accelerate in future.

4. The population was much poorer. GDP per capita, in real terms, was less than half of today's.[5] Yet the professional middle classes could afford more, in many areas. Private school fees were around 20% of median household income (and the majority of day places were paid for by the state through the direct grant scheme). Housing cost about half as much relative to earnings (and we were building more).[6] University, for the few that went, was free. And while 1974 and 1975 were terrible years for the economy, the previous decade had seen consistent growth and wage increases.

5. Many more women were housewives – which is precisely why Thatcher's housewife persona struck a chord. In the 1970s, half of households with children had only one adult working. Today it is a quarter.[7] The change has been particularly marked for those partnered with (back then we'd have said married to) higher-earning men.[8] And women in high-earning couples are not only much more likely to be in work, but to be in higher-earning jobs themselves.

6. The working and middle classes, and their children, were more upwardly mobile. There had been an explosion in the number

of professional jobs in the post-war period. Today, it is still true that around 80% of people end up in a job class different to their parents. But for every upwardly mobile person there is a downwardly mobile person. That makes life much, much more precarious for our graduates.[9]

7. Our jobs were different. Services counted for 60% of the economy vs 81% today. Manufacturing was 26% against less than 10% today.[10]

8. The adult population was a wartime population. Edward Heath had participated in the Normandy landings. Denis Healey was a beachmaster at Anzio. Many working-age adults were veterans, or had experienced (or been evacuated during) the Blitz. Further war seemed entirely plausible, not least because the Soviet Union remained a major threat. Military spending was, of course, much higher – 5.1% of GDP compared to 2.2% now.[11]

9. Religion was still a major part of life. Thatcher famously came from a non-conformist background. In the 1970s Methodist membership was still relatively high, if past its peak, and likewise for the Anglican Church. The majority had been brought up Anglican. In other words, when Thatcher quoted St Francis of Assisi on the steps of Downing Street – 'Where there is discord, may we bring harmony...' – people would actually have known who she was talking about. According to the British Social Attitudes survey, just 3% of those aged 18–25 today describe themselves as Anglican, compared to 40% of those aged 70 or older.[12] Attitudes were also more socially conservative in the 1970s.[13]

10. We watched, and discussed, the same events. There are still occasional moments that bring the nation together – the 2012 Olympics, or the Queen's funeral. But in 1974, more than a third of the popu-

lation – a full 21 million people – watched *Love Thy Neighbour*, a TV sitcom about a white working-class socialist living next door to a black Conservative.[14] The internet and social media have led to people finding content they like, not being stuck with whatever's on. That means, in turn, that we don't have the same cultural references. The BBC, in particular, is far less dominant than it once was.

In short, in 1974 the CPS was appealing to, and arguing to, a vastly different country. It was more homogenous in background, social behaviour and experience. While much poorer, it had seen major improvements in living standards and upward social mobility. A younger population meant that demands on the state, particularly in health and pensions, were much less.

The Britain of today, by contrast, is ageing, fractured and indeed fractious. It is also increasingly downwardly mobile, especially for those who cannot get on the housing ladder.

Many of the trends described above are global trends. Most of them are also irreversible. Whatever policy decisions ministers make on net migration, we will continue to become more ethnically diverse. We *will* continue to get older, which in turn will mean demands for more spending. We will continue to abandon religion. We will not start watching the same TV shows again.

This shift is reflected in changing public priorities, and it is here that policy becomes most significant – because our increasing age, and to an extent our increasing wealth, is changing what we want and expect. In 1974, a minuscule 3% of voters said that the NHS/health system was their main priority. Crime and education were minor concerns. The top issue, by miles, was inflation.[15] The biggest issue in terms of social policy? Trade unions.

Now? The economy undeniably matters, and inflation has recently reared its head (though it is plausible its importance will start to drop in the next year or two, barring major energy catastrophes in the Middle

East). But other than the economy, the top issues are the NHS and immigration – including, of course, illegal immigration.[16] Some 46% of people now choose health as a top concern.[17] Housing and the environment rank highly.

As we have got older and richer, we have changed what we care about.

So the challenge for the CPS, and organisations like it, is to tap into the same Thatcherite values – supporting your family, being rewarded for hard work and good behaviour, and yes, freedom to make your own decisions – in the context of much greater demands of the state. And as I will set out in the next section, it is implausible that we can do this by *reversing* the recent increases in the size of the state.

The choices we have made and the future demands of the state

In the last few decades, we have made some pivotal choices on spending, many as a consequence of our ageing society. We have:

- Increased pension benefits. Pensioner income has nearly doubled in real terms in the last few decades, and now matches – and on some measures exceeds – working age income. That is before you even start looking at assets.

- Increased spending on health (which predominantly goes on older people). In 1974 we spent 4% of GDP on the NHS. By 2010 it was 9.7%. Today, for all the discussion of austerity, it is 11.3%.

- Encouraged more inward migration, including low-skilled migration to feed the health and social care service (therefore including many migrants who are unlikely to be major net contributors in tax terms over their lifetime here).

The increased spending has been paid for in part by a large deficit, in part by tax rises and in part – particularly in recent years – by holding down investment in everything else. That includes our justice system (which has a huge backlog), policing (which is increasingly distrusted), prisons (which are highly overcrowded) and most notably our defence budget (which has more than halved since 1974).

And when politicians have had additional money, they have consistently chosen to spend it on further increases in not just the size but the scope of the welfare state – such as the expansion of in-work benefits in the 1990s and 2000s, or most recently through the expansion of childcare subsidies.

We have, of course, simultaneously refused to accept any of the trade-offs required – most obviously by preventing any building of housing or infrastructure to accommodate ever-increasing demand. To match the level of housing stock in the typical European country our size we would need four or five million more houses. Tory MPs recently rebelled over 300,000 a year.

At the moment, that fiscal picture looks set to get even worse. Partly because ageing is inexorable: models suggest that we will need a 4% real terms increase in NHS spending every year, just to keep service levels the same. The CPS, similarly, has calculated that we will need economic growth of 2.9% per year for the next half-century, just to maintain current levels of provision for the elderly.

But on top of that, we are also seeing large numbers of people exit the labour market while of working age, who are themselves requiring more from the NHS (including increasingly for mental health conditions preventing them from working). Many children are giving up on school for the same reason.

In short, an ever greater number of people are asking and will ask for state support, with an ever shrinking proportion of net contributors.

A larger state, but a worse state

Our ability to cope with these massive challenges is further diminished because, as well as making the state bigger, we have decided to make it ever more complex and centralised.[18]

In some ways the British state is less extensive than in the 1970s. Thanks to the efforts of the CPS and its allies, government no longer tries to direct economic activity through nationalised industries or prices and incomes policies. But complexity has multiplied in other, more insidious ways.

Legislation, for example, is increasingly difficult for MPs and peers to understand and evaluate, as it layers more and more onto pre-existing Acts. Our legal framework, including international laws, is sufficiently ambiguous that ministers frequently have no idea whether the decisions they are signing off will prove to be legal – because their officials cannot definitively tell them.

The creation of arm's-length organisations, including NHS England, means there is often nothing at the end of the lever that ministers try to pull. The desire for joined-up government creates endless write-rounds and snarling between different departments, which are usually resolved by an all-powerful but fundamentally inexpert Treasury. We have an ambition to procure huge infrastructure projects and technological programmes, and drive innovation, without beginning to have the expertise or longevity to achieve any of our aims.

The result is a state that is bigger but where pensions and healthcare are eating more and more of the pie. A smaller group of contributors, with more exiting the labour market. And a mass of sprawling complexity that means nothing appears to get delivered or improve.

It is not astonishing that the public are fed up. The most depressing example of this I can give is that, after the Conservatives giving far more than £350 million a week extra to the NHS in recent years – as promised on the side of that infamous bus – the public are utterly convinced that funding has been radically cut because hospital performance is so appalling.

Trust in politicians, therefore, is at rock bottom. In 1974, fewer than 40% of voters said that politicians were in it for themselves. Now it is more than 60%. For now, Britain remains a country where people trust each other – but not our leaders or institutions.[19]

And of course, as Danny Finkelstein put it so brilliantly, Labour are coming along to say: 'Britain is totally broken! Let's make sure we do nothing about it!'

Growth is vital, but it is not enough

As Ryan Bourne argues elsewhere in this collection, Conservatives need to return to thinking more about the supply side of our economy, as they did in the 1970s and 1980s – in particular, about how to build more homes and infrastructure and generate growth, which will in turn give us more money to spend on public services.

If we can't have a much smaller state in absolute terms, we may still be able to reduce its size as a percentage of GDP – but only with very punchy growth. For example, there are pretty convincing signs that you could unleash a substantial amount of economic activity by relaxing planning constraints in the South-East and particularly in the Oxford–Cambridge corridor – topics on which the CPS has been vocal.

If pro-growth reformers are to succeed politically, they will have to remember Thatcher's ability to ally economic policy to values. To me, the most important way to do that is to convince people that policy change will visibly and rapidly benefit *their* family, and reward hard work. New housing will help your children. Any attempt to generate more wealth will prioritise getting it to your family more quickly, so they can have a decent standard of living. If your kids put their head down and work hard, they'll be able to buy a home and afford a family.

It is notable that, even when older people express negative views about the younger generation, their own children and grandchildren tend to be excluded. We must use this fact more in policy. One of our major differences with the left, as Conservatives, has to be recognition of the family as the fundamental unit in society, admiration for familial responsibility and active encouragement of it.

But growth is not the main focus of this essay, even if it is a necessary precondition to progress. Because alongside such efforts, or even as a prerequisite, we need to restore trust in the state, in a way that is compatible with centre-right values – and which could also prevent it from increasing beyond any possible means to pay for it.

Towards a smarter state

Changes in economic policy will be insufficient if we on the centre-right cannot also restore a reputation for competence in the delivery of public services. Again, in my view, a radically smaller state is impossible given the accelerating changes in our population: even Thatcher increased spending on health. For example, while we may be able to slow the increases in pension spending, we are never going to reverse them. In addition, the reductions in defence spending will *have* to be reversed – you would have to be truly blind to expect the next 50 years to be as peaceful as the last.

So instead, we need the state to deliver more for its investment. Our only option is to make public services more competent and productive. To achieve that we need to consider four areas.

First, the overall system under which we govern and make public policy decisions. This has to become radically simpler, more decentralised and clearer in its aims. The concepts of bottom-up, choice-driven and more autonomous public services still have merit and it is a shame we have largely abandoned them. For example:

- You cannot micromanage a country of 70 million people from Whitehall. It is not a coincidence that small countries are always held up as the examples of good performance and innovation –

Singapore, Finland, Estonia. We need more decentralisation of decision-making, including away from the Treasury.

- That must be not only to local authorities and mayoralties. We also need to move operational decision-making down to lower layers. As the CPS warned, the decision to further integrate the NHS via Integrated Care Boards has created a byzantine nightmare of meetings and unclear accountability.[20] We must push decision-making closer to the end user. This also ought to help reduce waste, a source of extreme frustration for public sector workers as well as the public.

- We need a massive programme to clear up and simplify legislation. The test should be: can a minister rapidly master and evaluate the body of legislation that substantially informs his or her policy area? At the moment, only one department in Whitehall even has a full list of all the regulations it has imposed.

- We need to increase political accountability for policy decisions. The combination of operational independence and high central-isation of vast swathes of our public sector, including the NHS and the police, creates the worst of both worlds: bureaucracy and risk-aversion, and no ability to drive change. If a politician is accountable for an area, we need to be confident they have the ability to deliver.

- We need to recognise that our Civil Service – which in my experi-ence remains largely honest, decent and public-spirited – suited the model of a 19th-century government which made far fewer decisions, and which could therefore rely mostly on generalists. So we need to commit to Civil Service teams and ministers who stay in post long enough to be both expert and accountable. That means we will need to be willing to promote civil servants for staying in, and becoming better at, the same job. We will also have to pay properly for experts in areas that are in high market demand, including AI, and we will have to give them decision-making ability. If we don't want a ballooning pay bill, these decisions mean we will need fewer civil servants. Fewer, but better.

• We need to be willing to set a small number of very clear priorities for our public services. No system can operate with dozens of targets.

• We need to be willing to remove requirements from one part of the system in order to accommodate our priorities in other. For example, if we decide as a country that we need more public sector infrastructure – hospitals, schools, prisons – there should be zero time wasted on planning procedures.

Second, we need to understand better *what is going on*. Nothing is more fatal to trust than not knowing how many people are entering or leaving the country; a total uncertainty about whether people will be charged and imprisoned for crimes; or a lack of understanding of how many people are in the labour market, what they're doing and whether they're leaving.

My own view is that it is more than past time for ID cards – not just for the fluffy, acceptable but very real reason that they can support delivery of healthcare and services, but also so we know who is in the country, if they're working and what they're accessing. Robert Colvile has correctly identified a lack of databases as a core but very boring driver of government dysfunction. So we should have more of them, better connected.

Third, we unquestionably need to remove the barriers to technological adoption and experimentation. We have made some progress in innovation infrastructure in the last decade, not least via the creation of organisations such as the Francis Crick Institute; the establishment of ARIA (the Advanced Research and Invention Agency); and the example of Kate Bingham's vaccine taskforce. We need to be just as concerned with the dissemination of that innovation into the public sector. To do that, we need to remove some of the regulatory constraints against it.

Fourth, we need to be willing to have honest, decade-long conversations with the public. This is something that we Conservatives – and I include myself in this – have avoided like the plague.

People have no idea of the pressures we face because we haven't told them. In fact, we have actively deceived them. My personal bugbear is the use of 'National Insurance' payments to give the impression that their pension and healthcare have been funded. Which they duly believe. Maybe voters will refuse to allow long-term decisions and punish us for telling the truth. But have we really tried?

A small example of success

This may all seem impossible – even hopelessly naive. Yet we do have examples of success. Our education reforms in 2010, in which I was proud to play a small part as the founder of the New Schools Network, and later an adviser in No 10, demonstrated that it was possible to rapidly improve performance – as shown in a whole series of international tests – without major spending increases.

This was achieved through detailed reform of the curriculum, through the introduction of new schools and by allowing schools to take control of many of their own decisions. We used decentralisation down to individual schools, a greater degree of parental choice, and clarity about critical standards and targets.

Changes were delivered fast. It took 15 months from the general election to the first free schools opening for their first pupils. That included evaluating applications from prospective schools; creating the physical school; and having parents apply for their children. I recently explained this to some people who had only become involved in public policy in the last few years, and they couldn't believe it. Scleroticism has become hard-wired (this is even true within the free school programme, which has lost momentum).

The lessons from education, and the prerequisites for reform, are and were very similar to those I outline above, namely:

- First, and foremost, a clear idea of what the Department for Education wished to achieve, with a relatively small number of priorities and measures.

- The existence of outside organisations (not least the New Schools Network) relentlessly focused and motivated by the policy objective. This was accompanied by the use of outside experts, who were given clear roles within the Department for Education.

- Ministers who stayed put, most notably Nick Gibb, who as Schools Minister consistently drove through change over a number of years.

- A willingness to take some risk in the pursuit of a public policy objective.

- The reform agenda becoming a magnet for a series of extremely talented civil servants, who recognised that change was happening and wished to be part of it.

- A small enough team within the Department that rapid iteration was possible.

- Most importantly, a recognition that most of the hard work and innovation would come from teachers and from communities themselves. The market works because it relies on billions of individual actors. The state needs to get closer to the same principle.

I am not going to pretend that by following the recipe I outline here, those of us who want to fix the state will magic away all of our demographic and spending challenges. But at least we might look like we know what on earth we are trying to do – which, for both the CPS and for Thatcher, was essential.

If it finds itself in opposition, the Conservative Party will need to select key areas of the state and understand, in detail, how it wishes to reform them. Free schools worked, in large part, because the work was done before we entered government. They also worked because they reflected the values discussed at the beginning of the essay – allowing people the freedom to choose schools that were better for their family, that recognised aspiration as a virtue, and rewarded entrepreneurialism among teachers and head teachers.

Thatcher and her allies knew the importance of a free economy. But they also knew the importance of an effective state. The next great challenge for her successors will be to rebuild one.

Rachel Wolf is a Founding Partner at Public First. She co-authored the Conservative Party's election manifesto in 2019 and was previously education and innovation adviser to the Prime Minister at 10 Downing Street. She founded and ran the New Schools Network – the charity that helped develop and implement the Government's free schools programme.

16 Changing the Climate of Opinion: 10 Years of CapX

ALYS DENBY

'The climate of opinion… is shaped by the battle of ideas and by experience. If socialists, irrespective of their place in the spectrum, press their views vigorously, while we defer to what we believe to be the middle ground consensus, we lose the opportunity to achieve a more congenial climate for what will need doing in the future.'

In 1976, the Centre for Policy Studies published *Stranded on the Middle Ground?*, a collection of speeches by Keith Joseph.[1] In words that still resound today, Joseph attributed the country's profound economic and political afflictions – rampant inflation, sterling crises, the three-day week, trade union militancy, the collapse of successive governments – to the failure of the post-war consensus.

The 'middle ground', as he saw it, was determined by electoral expediency rather than any particular philosophy or popular feeling. It was obtained by splitting the difference between Labour and the Conservatives. And since Labour's position was always a compromise with its extreme fringe, the 'middle ground' had become a leftward ratchet towards socialism.

Joseph knew that dismantling this mechanism would take legwork – literally. In the lead-up to *Stranded on the Middle Ground?*, he had spent two years touring the country to make the moral case for capitalism, addressing 25,000 students at 60 public meetings at universities and polytechnics, and being shouted down on four of those occasions.

Those talks had a powerful effect: elsewhere in this collection, David Willetts writes evocatively about attending one as an undergraduate. And they were not the only example of communication and evangelisation being core to the CPS's early mission. In their famous paper 'Stepping Stones', John Hoskyns and Norman Strauss analysed the causes of Britain's political and economic dysfunction, concluding that unless union power was tamed, 'national recovery will be virtually impossible'. But the second half of the paper, written primarily by Strauss, was all about messaging – because nothing could be done unless the public were persuaded both of the negative role of the trade union leadership, and that those union barons could and should be taken on.

In other words, communication has always been central to the mission of the CPS. Keith Joseph, Margaret Thatcher and their allies understood from the beginning that they would require public understanding and support for their ideas if they were to make radical change.

In 2014, when the CPS launched CapX, the country had once again come to a crossroads. The financial crash of 2008 had led to profound economic disillusionment. As Tim Knox, then Director of the CPS, said at the time: 'Much has gone wrong with capitalism. We see cartelisation, we see large companies dominating countries, we see increasingly bad behaviour from banks, particularly, but also from energy companies and other cartel organisations. This is a long way from the free-market capitalism that we were founded to promote.'[2]

But it wasn't just the actions of industry that concerned many on the centre-right. It was the policy responses, too. Iain Martin, CapX's first Editor, says: 'The concern was, in the aftermath of the rescue of the banks, that there would be a perception that the state and giant interventions are always the answer.'[3]

At the same time, the internet was fundamentally changing the media landscape. The Guido Fawkes blog, launched in 2004, had shown that it wasn't just tabloids that could get big scoops and take political scalps. The Leveson Inquiry of 2011 had done real damage to the reputation of newspapers, which were also struggling financially as a result of online competition. All the frontier energy was in digital media start-ups and money was following, with sites like BuzzFeed and Vox receiving multi-billion-dollar valuations. Meanwhile a generation of journalists were learning to love the freedom and creativity the internet afforded them.

It was out of this intellectual atmosphere that CapX emerged: a news service that would bring readers original comment and analysis, as well as aggregated free-market thinking from around the world. It was utterly new, but completely consistent with what the CPS had always stood for.

CapX – the early years

Iain Martin had the idea for CapX while working at The Daily Telegraph, which was an early adopter of blogs alongside traditional op-eds. Indeed, for people of a certain age on the right, that section of the Telegraph website was a kind of prelapsarian online playground, where the likes of Norman Tebbit would interact – at length and in all seriousness – with anonymous users, their often ridiculous pseudonyms notwithstanding.

'Like many journalists in that period,' Martin recalls, 'I was introduced to this strange new world of the internet, instant publishing, and a different way of thinking about writing and communicating that wasn't constrained by the shapes on a page.' But he also worried about 'how people who believed in market liberalism within the rule of law and a robust state would get their argument heard in an increasingly frenetic media environment'.

Through discussion with George, now Baron Bridges – a former minister under John Major and board member of the CPS – he realised he would need funding and the backing of a major think tank. The CPS agreed to help facilitate both. Maurice Saatchi, then its Chairman, recalls: 'At that time, most people in the Conservative Party felt it had lost its intellectual bearing, and CapX struck all of us at the CPS as a very correct thing for us to be doing.'[4]

The offices at 57 Tufton Street were, back then, an incongruous environment from which to launch a digital start-up. Rachel Cunliffe, hired as an intern straight out of university to help with the launch, recalls being given a desk in an attic room with a leaky ceiling and coming across a cupboard filled with beverages earmarked for the 1997 general election, 16 years beyond their expiry date.[5]

Nonetheless Martin, Cunliffe, another intern called Zac Tate and CPS board member Susan Walton spent weeks sitting around the boardroom table thinking and talking – much of the discussion centring around the term 'capitalism' itself. 'It's a word that a lot of people regard as ugly and that was invented by enemies of business,' says Martin. 'But in the end we decided to embrace it and to own it, because in 100 years no one has invented a better term.'

He was clear, though, that the site wouldn't shy away from criticism of markets or claim that they worked in every circumstance. Instead, he wanted to advocate for a system that could both command popular appeal and promote prosperity for the many, not just the elites. So they settled on 'popular capitalism' as the site's animating ethos.

Next came the name and logo, though recollections about the origins of the 'X' in 'CapX' vary. Cunliffe says that the 'X' was meant to represent markets via a visual allusion to supply and demand curves. Lord Saatchi, on the other hand, says it had more to do with technology and the future – and that the CPS recognised the potency of the letter long before Elon Musk. Everyone involved agrees, though, that the name seemed to capture what they were trying to do. The bold, monochrome aesthetic of the site – which has been much imitated since – flowed from there, and Martin gives much credit to Lord Saatchi's 'marketing and branding genius'.

CapX was launched on 16 June 2014 at the Margaret Thatcher Conference on Liberty – the first in what has now become an annual series of high-profile conferences to celebrate the CPS's founder. The first ever daily CapX newsletter featured articles on the economies of India and France, a piece by Patience Wheatcroft on Pfizer's failed takeover of AstraZeneca and one from Tim Montgomerie on the rise of 'BoreCons'[6] – which, given the upheaval of the subsequent decade, now reads like wishful thinking.

The original promotional materials emphasised the site's function as an aggregator of free-market content from across the web. The idea of using machine learning to scour the internet for information on a certain theme, which would then be curated by editors, was well ahead of its time.

But as technology changed and CapX's audience grew, it became clear that original comment would be its main selling point.

Early articles often had a defiant, anti-establishment tone – with titles like 'Popular Capitalism, Now!' and 'Is the Pope a Capitalist?'.[7] There was even a wine column from Will Lyons and watch reviews[8] – presumably published on the assumption that readers interested in capitalism would also be keen consumers of luxury goods. In articles like 'Are Cats Libertarians?' and 'JRR Tolkien and the Economics of Middle Earth', CapX found a way to make free markets funny.[9]

But the core offer was always astute comment and analysis of the big political and economic stories of the day from great writers. And there has been plenty to write about since 2014.

Making history

The American political scientist Francis Fukuyama famously referred to the triumph of liberal democracy at the end of the Cold War as 'the end of history'. It now feels as though history has restarted. And looking back, CapX – founded in the year Russia snatched Crimea from Ukraine – came along at just the right time.

Ever since, it has been a platform for writers to debate, analyse and – in its own way – shape a period of extraordinary change, in Britain and around the world.

The launch of CapX was swiftly followed by the 2015 general election and the Brexit referendum. While the newspapers and other media outlets tended to either focus on personalities – Nigel Farage vs the Establishment – or repeat Treasury scaremongering,[10] CapX offered far more nuanced analysis. 'So many Remainers were surprised by the referendum result,' says Cunliffe. 'But I wasn't, because working at CapX, I'd read some extremely compelling arguments.' She adds:

'I also understood something which is very apparent now, that there are two very, very different cases for Brexit. One is the populist, nationalistic argument for lower immigration and more money for the NHS, which won votes in the Red Wall. And the other is about free trade, cutting red tape and making Britain a world leader. We had really eloquent writers on both sides.'

For Robert Colvile, who took over as CapX's Editor in 2016, the election of Jeremy Corbyn as Labour leader was a catalysing incident. 'After the 2015 election Labour had chosen this guy who, whether on domestic or foreign policy, believed all the things that were most alien to human flourishing, most alien to everything we know about how an economy works, and most alien to our values,' he says.[11] A fruitful source of content for CapX during this period was simply exposing things Corbyn had done and said. For example in 'What Corbyn Really

Thinks about Foreign Policy', Colvile mined the Corbyn archives for quotes on his enthusiastic support for Hugo Chavez and the Cuban dictatorship, while in 'How can Labour's Leader be in Thrall to Marx?' Daniel Hannan examined the lethal legacy of the far-left's favourite philosopher.[12] 'You came into the office every day knowing you were doing God's work,' says Colvile.

Corbyn was, thankfully, defeated at the 2019 election – only to thrust CapX, and the country, into another huge debate over the role and purpose of the state. The Covid lockdowns of 2020 and 2021 were the biggest experiment in state coercion ever conducted in Britain, and the Government imposed them with little challenge from much of the media.

By this point CapX was in the hands of a new generation of talent – John Ashmore had succeeded Oliver Wiseman, who succeeded Colvile's deputy and fellow Telegraph veteran Sally Chatterton. 'We took the line that it was important to preserve as much personal freedom as possible while protecting lives,' says Ashmore, 'and that innovation and technology would be the means by which we defeated the virus.'[13]

While this premise was shared by CapX writers, many disagreed on the way to achieve it. During the vaccine rollout, for example, Alex Morton argued for New Zealand-style border closures, whereas I wrote that restrictions should be lifted faster.[14] 'It was a very frenetic time, but we tried to balance competing, legitimate views, and act as a voice of reason amid the madness,' says Ashmore. 'We had lots of anti-lockdown pieces, but also pieces from those making a pragmatic case for some of the measures – we wanted CapX to be a place where those ideas could be properly debated, rather than simply saying we were "pro" or "anti" one course of action or another.'

Why we need CapX now

That ambition, to be the marketplace of ideas, still motivates CapX a decade on. Today it is read by many of the most influential people on the right. Michael Gove has said, 'I always feel better for the arrival of the CapX email, I'm always stimulated, intrigued, provoked and better informed.' Lord Frost regards it as 'one of the daily reads that I regard as indispensable'. And Maurice Saatchi says, 'in terms of the writing and the provocative ideas, it's better than The Economist'. Many less well known but still powerful and influential people keep an eye on CapX too. One of our Labour-leaning writers did such a good job setting out the kind of arguments Keir Starmer should be making that he got hired as his speechwriter.

CapX also reaches a far wider audience and, much like the Telegraph website back in the 2010s, is an important touchstone for a newer generation of right-wingers. This is all the more important given the culture at universities today, where there is often a steep social cost to being an openly right-wing student or academic (it is hard to imagine a modern Keith Joseph being shouted down only four times).

It is an enormous compliment to the site that it now has many imitators. CapX can also be immensely proud of the talent that has passed through its doors. Cunliffe is now Associate Political Editor of the New Statesman. Chatterton left to become one of the founding team at UnHerd, which she has edited for the past five years. Former intern Olivia Utley is now Political Correspondent at GB News. Wiseman is working for The Free Press in the Washington, DC. And of course Colvile is now Director of the Centre for Policy Studies.

But despite such success, the public has not become axiomatically more receptive to our ideas. Aside from the statistical blips of the pandemic years, 2014 was the last time UK GDP growth topped 3%. Meanwhile, the tax burden is at its highest level in over 70 years. As Ryan Bourne notes in his essay in this collection, the Thatcher revolution now looks like something of an interlude between two periods of decline and declinism.

As a result, the Tories are heading into a general election with dire poll ratings and a country that, for many, seems no more conservative than it was in 2010, despite 14 years of Conservative-led government.

So on the 10th anniversary of CapX and the 50th of the Centre for Policy Studies, it feels like Britain is approaching another inflection point.

Returning to *Stranded on the Middle Ground?*, Keith Joseph wrote: 'The two world wars impelled society towards interventionism and socialism… the militarisation of society entails confiding vast additional powers to government, legitimises these powers in the name of patriotism, indeed of national survival.'

The pandemic has once again convinced people that there is a romance in the co-ordination of state powers. For many people, especially younger people, equality now matters far more than than freedom. At the same time, the mistakes of Liz Truss' brief premiership have done much to discredit her tax-cutting, deregulating vision.

Yet for all her faults, much of her analysis of Britain's economic ailments was correct. And it is a sort of perverse tribute to her that even Keir Starmer now talks about the importance of growth – though he has less to say about how he plans to get it.

CapX's mission, then, remains as necessary and as urgent as ever. While the left peddle easy fallacies about fairness, the right must argue that individual liberty is the surest path to collective prosperity. While they buy into utopian fictions about a perfectible society, we know that only the market can balance competing interests. Our opponents think they know how we must live our lives; we don't tell others how they should live theirs.

But it is precisely because these arguments are difficult, even at times counter-intuitive, that they must be constantly remade. That is what CapX will keep doing, for the next 10 years and beyond.

Alys Denby was Deputy Editor of CapX from 2020 to 2023, and Editor of CapX from 2023 to 2024.

Notes

....

Introduction: A Conservative Revolution?

1 M. Thatcher, 'Speech to Centre for Policy Studies (AGM)'
(16 July 1991), Margaret Thatcher Foundation Website
[https://www.margaretthatcher.org/] (hereafter *TFW*).

2 M. Thatcher, as quoted in D.S. Broder, 'The Resurgent Right',
The Washington Post (28 April 1979).

3 M. Thatcher, 'Speech of Tribute to Keith Joseph (All Souls
Commemoration)' (3 June 1995), *TFW*.

4 M. Thatcher, 'Interview for Woman's Own ("no such thing [as society]")'
(23 September 1987), *TFW*.

5 K. Joseph, 'Draft Prospectus ("Centre for Policy Studies Limited")'
(7 June 1974), *TFW*.

3 What was Thatcherism?

1 M. Thatcher, 'Speech to Conservative Central Council'
(15 March 1975), Margaret Thatcher Foundation Website [https://
www.margaretthatcher.org/] (hereafter *TFW*); and see R. Saunders,
'"Crisis? What Crisis?" Thatcherism and the Seventies', in B. Jackson &
R. Saunders (eds.), *Making Thatcher's Britain* (2012), p.29; R. Saunders,
'The Many Lives of Margaret Thatcher', The English Historical Review
132 (14 June 2017), p.651; M. Bailey & P. Cowley, 'Thatcherism: Not
Born in Birmingham', ConservativeHome (16 March 2015) [http://
www.conservativehome.com/platform/2015/03/matthew-bentley-and-
philip-cowley-thatcherism-not-born-in-birmingham.html].

2 S. Hall, 'The Great Moving Right Show', Marxism Today (January 1979), pp.14–20; D. Marquand, 'The Paradoxes of Thatcherism', in R. Skidelsky (ed.), *Thatcherism* (1988), p.160; A. Mitchell, *Four Years in the Death of the Labour Party* (1983), p.15.

3 For a good survey of this colossal subject, mercifully free of political-science jargon, see Saunders, 'The Many Lives of Margaret Thatcher'.

4 N. Lawson, *The View from No. 11: Memoirs of a Tory Radical* (1992 (1993)), p.64; 'TV Interview for BBC1 *Panorama*' (8 June 1987), *TFW*.

5 I. Gilmour, *Dancing with Dogma: Britain under Thatcherism* (1993), p.11; W. Wyatt, *The Journals of Woodrow Wyatt*, vol. 1 (1998), p.585; E.H.H. Green, *Thatcher* (2003), p.33; G. Stewart, *Bang! A History of Britain in the 1980s* (2013), p.61.

6 M. Thatcher, 'Speech to Conservative Party Conference' (14 October 1983), *TFW*; and see Green, *Thatcher*, pp.21–54; E.H.H. Green, *Ideologies of Conservatism: Conservative Political Ideas in the Twentieth Century* (2002), pp.214–39; R. Vinen, *Thatcher's Britain: The Politics and Social Upheaval of the 1980s* (2009) p.288; Stewart, *Bang!*, pp.61–2.

7 'TV Interview for BBC1 *Panorama*' (8 June 1987), *TFW*; N. Lawson, 'The New Conservatism: Lecture to the Bow Group' (4 August 1980).

8 B. Jessop, K. Bonnett, S. Bromley & T. Ling, 'Authoritarian Populism, Two Nations, and Thatcherism', New Left Review 147 (1984), pp.32–60; Vinen, *Thatcher's Britain*, pp.4, 275–6; 'Speech to Greater London Young Conservatives: Iain Macleod Lecture, "Dimensions of Conservatism"' (4 July 1977), *TFW*; Saunders, 'Thatcherism and the Seventies', pp.28–9.

9 M. Thatcher, 'Speech of Tribute to Keith Joseph (All Souls Commemoration)' (3 June 1995), *TFW*.

10 C. Moore, *Margaret Thatcher: The Authorized Biography, Volume One: Not for Turning* (2013), p.302; Vinen, *Thatcher's Britain*, pp.282, 57; *The Times* (31 March 1983); 'TV Interview for BBC *Campaign '79*' (27 April 1979), *TFW*; *New York Times* (29 April 1979); J. Coles, 'Appreciation of Margaret Thatcher' (c.14 June 1984), *TFW*; H. Young, *This Blessed Plot: Britain and Europe from Churchill to Blair* (1998), p.307.

11 J. Ranelagh, *Thatcher's People: An Insider's Account of the Politics, the Power and the Personalities* (1991), p.71.

12 D. Cannadine, 'Apocalypse When? British Politicians and British "Decline" in the Twentieth Century', in P. Clarke & C. Trebilcock (eds.), *Understanding Decline: Perceptions and Realities of British Economic Performance* (1997), p.262; M. Thatcher, *The Downing Street Years* (1993), p.15; 'Message to the People of Britain' (16 April 1979), *TFW*; 'Speech to Conservative Rally in Bolton' (1 May 1979), *TFW*; 'TV Interview for BBC *Campaign '79*' (27 April 1979), *TFW*.

13 K. Joseph, 'Solving the Union Problem is the Key to Britain's Recovery' (1979), p.5.

14 Thatcher, 'Tribute to Keith Joseph'.

15 Her ghostwriters were guilty of a slight misquotation. What Pitt actually said was: 'My Lord, I am sure I can save this country, and no one else can.'

16 J. Aitken, *Margaret Thatcher* (2013), p.268; Lord Hailsham, *The Dilemma of Democracy: Diagnosis and Prescription* (1978), pp.15, 22; I. Trewin (ed.), *The Hugo Young Papers*, pp.120–1; Green, *Thatcher*, p.55; Thatcher, *The Downing Street Years*, p.10. Saunders, 'Thatcherism and the Seventies', pp.30–31, is very good on all this.

17 C. Moore, *Everything She Wants* (2016), pp.6–7; 'TV Interview for De Wolfe Productions' (30 December 1982), *TFW*.

18 Moore, *Everything She Wants* (2016), pp.8, 6; Moore, *Not for Turning*, pp.302, 577, 300; J. Campbell, *The Iron Lady* (2009), p.250; M. Parris, *Chance Witness* (2002), p.204; 'TV Interview for BBC1 *Panorama*' (8 June 1987), *TFW*.

19 F. Mount, *Cold Cream* (2008), pp.287–8; '1979 Election Address: "The Britain I Want to See"' (11 April 1979), *TFW*.

20 'Notes for Conference Speech ("Thoughts on the Moral Case")' (3 October 1979), *TFW*.

21 Daily Telegraph (18 September 1984), quoted in H. Young, *One of Us: A Biography of Margaret Thatcher* (1990), p.352; 'Speech in Finchley (Adoption)' (11 April 1979), *TFW*; 'Speech at St Lawrence Jewry' (4 March 1981), *TFW*; The Times (5 March 1981); and see M. Grimley, 'Thatcherism, Morality and Religion', in Jackson & Saunders (eds.), *Making Thatcher's Britain*, pp.84, 88–9.

22 E. Filby, *God and Mrs Thatcher: The Battle for Britain's Soul* (2015), pp.9, 14–15, 21; Moore, *Not for Turning*, p.349; Moore, *Everything She Wants*, p.447; Parris, *Chance Witness*, pp.186–7.

23 Saunders, 'The Many Lives of Margaret Thatcher', p.653; *News of the World* (20 September 1981), quoted in Stewart, *Bang!*, p.62. For a clip of the *Nationwide* interview, which went out on 20 April 1979, see the first episode of *The 80s* (BBC2, 2016).

24 B. Harrison, *Finding a Role? The United Kingdom 1970–1990* (2010), pp.140, 406; Moore, *Not for Turning*, p.308; J. Lawrence & F. Sutcliffe-Braithwaite, 'Margaret Thatcher and the Decline of Class Politics', in Jackson and Saunders (eds.), *Making Thatcher's Britain*, pp.134–5, 142.

25 Lawrence & Sutcliffe-Braithwaite, 'Margaret Thatcher and the Decline of Class Politics', pp.139–43; 'Speech to Conservative Trade Unionists Conference' (11 March 1978), *TFW*.

26 J. Campbell, *Margaret Thatcher*, vol. 1, *The Grocer's Daughter* (2000), p.3; Green, *Thatcher*, p.18; A. Sampson, *The Changing Anatomy of Britain* (1982), p.41; *New York Times* (29 April 1979); Saunders, 'The Many Lives of Margaret Thatcher', pp.641–2; 'Remarks on Becoming Prime Minister' (4 May 1979), *TFW*.

4 Alfred Sherman and the Fanatical Lamas

1 A. Fisher, *Must History Repeat Itself?* (Churchill Press, 1974), p.103.

2 F. Hayek, 'The Intellectuals and Socialism', The University of Chicago Law Review 16, no. 3 (1949), pp.417–33.

3 J. Hoskyns, 'Foreword', in A. Sherman, *Paradoxes of Power: Reflections on the Thatcher Interlude* (Imprint Academic, 2007), p.1.

4 M. Thatcher, *The Path to Power* (HarperCollins, 1995), p.251.

5 LSE Archives, London, Cockett [hereafter LSE/Cockett], 2/3, A. Sherman, 'Counting the Cost of New Towns' (10/8/73).

6 R. Cockett, *Thinking the Unthinkable: Think-Tanks and the Economic Counter-Revolution 1931–83* [hereafter, *Thinking*] (Fontana Press, 1995), p.232.

7 M. Halcrow, *A Single Mind* (Macmillan, 1989), p.59.

8   D. Kavanagh, *Thatcherism and British Politics: The End of Consensus?* (Oxford University Press, 1987), p.96.

9   LSE/CPS/6/2, 'Speaking Modules' (23/3/79).

10 J. Hoskyns, *Just in Time* (Aurum Press, 2000), p.18.

11 M. Garnett, 'Editor's Foreword', in Sherman, *Paradoxes*, p.11.

12 D. Wood, '"Mystery" man behind new Tory thought', *The Times* (12/6/78).

13 F. Mount, 'An Amazing Coincidence', The Spectator (3/6/78).

14 LSE/Cockett/2/3, 'Confessions of a man of ideas fallen among party politicians', Guardian (29/6/81).

15 Cockett, *Thinking*, p.241. N.B. Compare use of the phrase 'good intentions' with another critical article Sherman wrote in 1973, 'The Subsidised Road of Good Intentions'.

16 H. Young, *One of Us* (Macmillan, 1991), p.89.

17 See LSE/CPS/6/1. To read about what Sherman calls the Edgbaston 'affair' see Sherman, *Paradoxes*, pp.55–60.

18 Cockett, *Thinking*, p.255.

19 Mount, 'An Amazing Coincidence'.

20 Bodleian Library , Oxford, Conservative Party Archive [hereafter BOD/CPA] KJ/18/9, Letter: KJ to Angus Maude (cc. Chris Patten) (30/5/77).

21 BOD/KJ/18/8, Letter: Joseph to Chris Patten (7/1/76).

22 BOD/KJ/18/8, Letter: KJ to Chris Patten (14/1/76).

23 Conservative Central Office, the forerunner of today's Conservative Campaign Headquarters (CCHQ).

24 Hoskyns, *Just in Time*, pp.6–17.

25 Another businessman, Nigel Vinson, was also integral to the success of the CPS financially and operationally.

26 Royal Holloway, London, Sherman Papers [hereafter RHL/AS] I/19, Letter: Sherman to Joseph (October 1975).

27 Hoskyns, *Just in Time*, pp.17–18.

28 Churchill Archives Centre, The Papers of Sir John Hoskyns, 1974–82 [hereafter CAC/JH], GBR/0014/HOSK1, Norman Strauss, 'A Simple Way to Look at Slogans' (26/7/76).

29 LSE/Cockett/1/10, N. Strauss, 'The Need for New Data' (3/8/76).

30 LSE/CPS/2/2, Letter: Simon Webley to Joseph (8/3/77).

31 LSE/Cockett/1/10, Memo: Sherman to Joseph (22/4/75).

32 CAC/JH/GBR/0014/HOSK1, Letter: Hoskyns to Keith Joseph (12/6/77).

33 Cockett, *Thinking*, p.242.

34 Young, *One of Us*, p.88.

35 Margaret Thatcher Foundation Archive, THCR 5/1/2/153, 'Briefing Notes for Walden Interview' (15/9/77).

36 Thatcher, *Path to Power*, p.424.

37 Cockett, *Thinking*, p.265.

38 Young, *One of Us*, p.113.

39 J. Hoskyns & N. Strauss, 'Stepping Stones' (CPS, 1977) p.3.

40 Ibid., p.37.

41 Hoskyns & Strauss, 'Stepping Stones'.

42 BOD/KJ/8/1, 'The Policy Group Work' (2/3/76).

43 Sherman, *Paradoxes*, p.29.

44 LSE/CPS/2/2, Letter: Martin Wassell to Joseph (13/9/75).

45 F. Mount, *Cold Cream: My Early Life and Other Mistakes* (Bloomsbury, 2008), p.303.

46 BOD/CRD/D/8/16, Letter: Adam Ridley to Heath (3/12/74).

47 Mount, *Cold Cream*, p.304.

48 Thatcher, *Path to Power*, p.251.

49 LSE/CPS/6/1(15), Speech Draft: 'Tory Vision' (21/12/77).

50 RHL/AS, Letter: Thatcher to Sherman (20/10/77).

51 Mount, *Cold Cream*, p.303.

52 A Tibetan fortress, manned by warrior-monks.

53 BOD/CRD/D/8/16, 'The centre can hold them', Guardian (26/9/80).

54 D. Wood, '"Mystery" man'.

55 Sherman, 'Confessions of a man', p.9.

56 LSE/CPS/2/2, Memo: Martin Wassell to Joseph (18/12/74).

57 CPS: 'Stepping Stones', p.270.

58 Ibid., p.S-1.

59 LSE/CPS/6/2, 'Economic Policy' (29/3/79).

60 LSE/CPS/6/3, 'Thatcher's Party Election Broadcast' (30/4/79).

61   BOD/CRD/D/8/1, Letter: Dermot Gleeson to Lord Thorneycroft (16/5/79).

62   LSE/CPS/6/1, 'All of a sudden Margaret Thatcher looks like a real prime minister', The Sunday Times (24/7/77).

63   RHL/AS/SPEECHWRITING 10 [Box 1]/1/1, Minutes: Speechwriters Conference (23/4/79).

64   Hoskyns, Just in Time, p.352.

65   RHL/AS/MISC 11[Box 2]/7/2, Letter: Hugh Thomas to Sherman (3/10/83).

66   Sherman memo, quoted in Cockett, Thinking, p.318.

67   RHL/AS/MISC 11[Box 2]/7/7, Memo: Alfred Sherman to Ian Gow (10/5/83).

68   Ibid., 320.

69   Hoskyns, Just in Time, p.99.

6 Did Monetarism Work?

1   K. Marx, The Communist Manifesto (1848).

2   Thanks in no small part to Beatrice and Sidney Webb's Soviet Communism: A New Civilisation? (Longmans, 1935). Gulags, purges, ethnic cleansings and the Holodomor genocide in Ukraine were not widely known about at the time.

3   C. Kennedy, 'Monetary Policy', in David Worswick & Peter Ady (eds.), The British Economy in the Nineteen-Fifties (Oxford University Press, 1962), p.317.

4   Central Statistical Office, Economic Trends: Annual Supplement (Her Majesty's Stationery Office, 1985), p.146.

5   E. Heath, as quoted in: '1972: Pay and price freeze aims to curb inflation', BBC (6 November 1972) [http://news.bbc.co.uk/onthisday/hi/dates/stories/november/6/newsid_2538000/2538623.stm].

6   The original 'teenage scribbler'. Compare the Chancellor in 1986: 'I would not take too much notice of teenage scribblers in the City who jump up and down in an effort to get press attention.' N. Lawson, as quoted in City AM Reporter, 'Nigel Lawson in 10 of his most memorable quotes', City AM (4 April 2023).

7 For further discussion, see T. Congdon, *Monetarism: An Essay in Definition* (CPS, 1978).

8 Alan Budd was a founding member of the Bank of England's Monetary Policy Committee in 1997, when he was also knighted. Terry Burns became a life peer in 1998, after serving as chief economic adviser to the Treasury and head of the Government Economic Service from 1980 to 1991, and Permanent Secretary of HM Treasury from 1991 to 1998.

9 The reasons for this are too complex and controversial to include within the scope of the present essay.

7 The Economics of Thatcherism: Paradigm Shift or Interlude?

1 C. Burns, 'Margaret Thatcher's Greatest Achievement: New Labour', ConservativeHome (11 April 2008).

2 A. Sherman, *Paradoxes of Power: Reflections on the Thatcher Interlude* (Imprint Academic, 2007).

3 S.R. Letwin, *The Anatomy of Thatcherism* (Transaction Publishers, 1992 (Routledge, 2018)).

4 See for example, NERA, *The Performance of Privatisation Vol. III: Privatisation and Efficiency* (CPS, 1996).

5 A. Tyrie, 'After the Age of Abundance: It's the Economy' (CPS, November 2011).

6 M. Wolf, 'Why radical reform of urban planning is essential', Financial Times (16 May 2021).

7 M. Feeney & R. Colvile (eds.), *Justice for the Young* (CPS, November 2023).

8 K. Joseph, Speech at Upminster, 22 June 1974.

8 Back to the 1970s?

1 M. Cowling, *1867: Disraeli, Gladstone and Revolution: The Passing of the Second Reform Bill* (Cambridge University Press, 1967), pp.2–6, 340.

2 M. Cowling, *The Impact of Labour, 1920–1924* (Cambridge University Press, 1971), pp.3–12.

3 M. Cowling, *The Impact of Hitler: British Politics and British Policy, 1933–1940* (Cambridge University Press, 1975), pp.1–10.

9 Reinventing Conservatism, Then and Now

1   C. Moore, *Margaret Thatcher: The Authorized Biography, Volume One: Not for Turning* (Allen Lane, 2013).

2   N. Lawson 'The British Experiment (The Mais Lecture)' (18 June 1984), Margaret Thatcher Foundation Website [https://www.margaretthatcher.org/document/109504].

3   See for example, M. Feeney & R. Colvile (eds.), *Justice for the Young* (CPS, November 2023).

10 Maggie, Markets and Me

1   Although in his monumental biography of Thatcher, Charles Moore places the discussion in Keith Joseph's parliamentary office.

2   D. Jay, *The Socialist Case* (Faber and Faber, 1937), p.317.

3   A very full account of this is in R. Cockett, *Thinking the Unthinkable: Think-Tanks and the Economic Counter-Revolution 1931–1983* (HarperCollins, 1994). The final chapter is subtitled 'Triumph and Despair 1979–1983', which conveys very well how some of the frustrated radicals thought it had all gone wrong.

4   A. Sykes & C. Robinson, 'Current Choices: Good Ways and Bad Ways to Privatise Electricity' (CPS, 1987); R. Albon, 'Privatise the Post: Steps Towards a Competitive Service' (CPS, 1987); A. Henney, 'Privatise Power: Restructuring the Electricity Supply Industry' (CPS, 1987); A. Sykes & C. Robinson, 'Privatise Coal: Achieving International Competitiveness' (CPS, 1991); A. Gritten, *Reviving the Railways: A Victorian Future* (CPS, 1988).

5   J. Peet, 'Healthy Competition: How to Improve the NHS' (CPS, 1987).

6   J. Marenbon, *English Our English – The New Orthodoxy Examined* (CPS, 1987).

7   Z. Brzezinski, *From Eastern Europe back to Central Europe* (Collier Books, 1988), p.12.

8   O. Letwin, *Hearts and Minds* (Biteback, 2017).

9   M. Howe & M. Walsh, 'Recommendations for the Intergovernmental Conference: Opposing Views' (CPS, 1996).

10 G. Urban, *Diplomacy and Disillusion at the Court of Margaret Thatcher* (Blackwells, 1996).

11 G. Himmelfarb, 'Victorian Values and Twentieth Century Condescension' (CPS, 1987).

12 R. Harris, *The Conservative Community: The Roots of Thatcherism and its Future* (CPS, 1989).

11 Turning Policy into Action

1 The question of 'What is a thing?' has exercised many of the finest philosophers of the Western canon. A quick Google search will show that Kant, Schopenhauer and Heidegger have all debated the question, at some length. But in this context, a 'thing' is simply used in its primary definition of a 'material thing that can be seen and touched', as opposed to that of an abstract or metaphysical entity, however 'real' that entity may or may not be.

2 Whether or not we are at a similar stage today is left to the reader to decide.

3 Synthetic phonics involves teaching children to decode words by breaking them down into small units of sound (called phonemes). In turn, these phonemes are represented in written language using groups of letters called graphemes. Children can then be taught to blend all the sounds together as a way of reading the entire word. While this method of teaching can be repetitive, it has the advantage that it works.

4 For more information on reading skills in the 1990s, see: DfE, *The National Strategies 1997–2011* (2011).

5 Department for Education and Skills, *Independent Review of the Teaching of Early Reading* (March 2006).

6 'The Government must learn from phonics fiasco', Daily Telegraph (4 June 2005).

7 How many children? A rough calculation: there are roughly 700,000 children in each school year. Since 2012, that means 7.7 million children have passed through the system. If only 58% of them could read well in 2012, that means there were 294,000 with inadequate reading skills. Today, 79% read well, meaning that 147,000 have inadequate reading

skills. A difference of 147,000 children a year over 11 years means that over 1,600,000 are now able to read well. This calculation takes no account of the improvement in the overall reading ability of children through synthetic phonics.

8   Nick Gibb, as quoted in DfE, *More Primary School Children Reach Reading Standards* (October 2023).

9   Liberal Democrats, *Liberal Democrat Manifesto 2010* (2010).

10 A. Seely, *Income Tax: Increases in the Personal Allowance since 2010* (House of Commons Library, 15 November 2018).

11 For example, this millennium the CPS was at the forefront of such policies as free schools, the Osborne Corporation Tax and pension reforms, the abolition of the 50p tax rate, automatic enrolment in private pensions and privatising the Green Investment Bank, among many other policies. In addition to developing such policies, we were also among the first to sound the alarm bell about the impact of unrestricted immigration on poorer households, the hubris of Gordon Brown's claims to have eliminated 'boom and bust' and the steady rise in the proportion of households who receive more in benefits than they pay in tax.

12 This comparison was first made by Mark Littlewood about the Institute of Economic Affairs.

12 Keeping the Flame Alive

1   D. Willetts & R. Forsdyke, 'After the Landslide: Learning the Lessons of 1906 and 1945' (CPS, September 1999).

2   D. Cameron, 'speech' (29 June 2005); *For the Record* (William Collins, 2019), p.63.

3   M. d'Ancona, 'The First Modernisers: The Centre for Policy Studies: Past & Future' (CPS, December 1999).

4   M. Thatcher, *The Path to Power* (HarperCollins, 1995), p.253.

5   C. Moore, *Margaret Thatcher: The Authorized Biography, Volume One: Not for Turning* (Allen Lane, 2013), p.255. (On sockets, as on most things, Mrs Thatcher had strong views: 'Simon Webley, one of the CPS's moving spirits, remembered her holding up the wires and exclaiming, "The

brown one is supposed to be the live one. That is absolutely ridiculous. Brown is for earth.'")

6 Conservative Party manifesto, *You Can Only Be Sure with the Conservatives* (1997).

7 D. Cameron, 'speech at Chalvedon School and Sixth Form College, Basildon, Essex' (9 January 2006), cited in The Guardian (9 January 2006).

8 Lord Blackwell, 'Three Cheers for Selection: How Grammar Schools Help the Poor' (CPS, December 2006), p.6.

9 Ibid., pp.10, 14.

10 *BBC News* website (29 May 2007).

11 The Guardian (9 January 2006).

12 CPS press release (13 July 2011).

13 Conservative History Journal, vol. I, issue 7 (Autumn 2007), pp.31–2.

14 All of these – bar Hayek, Marx and Lenin – had already been cited by October 1975, thanks to Peter Vansittart's *The Ancient Mariner and The Old Sailor: Delights and Uses of the English Language* (CPS, 1975).

15 Ibid., p.28.

16 W.M. Thackeray, 'Nil Nisi Bonum' (1862).

17 G. Osborne, 'speech at the annual Trustees' Dinner, British Museum' (2 November 2022).

18 M. Thatcher, foreword to *History, Capitalism and Freedom* (CPS, 1979), p.v.

19 H. Thomas, *History, Capitalism and Freedom* (CPS, 1979), pp.2–3.

20 Ibid., p.6.

21 The Daily Telegraph (19 March 1990); DfE, 'National Curriculum in England: History Programmes of Study' (11 September 2013); DCMS, '*Guidance* for Custodians on How to Deal with Commemorative Heritage Assets that have Become Contested' (5 October 2023).

22 K. Amis, *An Arts Policy?* (CPS, 1979), p.9.

23 Ibid., p.10.

24 Ibid., p.8.

25 Ibid., p.7.

26 See for example, DCMS, *Creative Industries Sector Vision: A Joint Plan to Drive Growth, Build Talent and Develop Skills* (14 June 2023).

27 To echo the characterisation used by Sir Alfred Sherman, one of the
    founders of the CPS, who died during my time there.

13 50 Years of Fighting for Freedom

1 N. Tebbit, *Unfinished Business* (1991).

2 M. Thatcher, 'Speech to Junior Carlton Club Political Council' (4
   May 1976), Margaret Thatcher Foundation Website [https://www.
   margaretthatcher.org/document/103017] (hereafter *TFW*).

3 M. Thatcher, 'Speech to Greater London Young Conservatives (Iain
   Macleod Memorial Lecture – "Dimensions of Conservatism")' (4 July
   1977), *TFW* [https://www.margaretthatcher.org/document/103411].

4 CPS, *Policies of Thatcherism* (CPS, 1989).

5 M. Thatcher, 'Speech to Christian Democratic Union Conference'
   (25 May 1976), *TFW* [https://www.margaretthatcher.org/
   document/103034].

6 Thatcher, 'Iain Macleod Memorial Lecture'.

15 What Next? Fixing the State

1 J. Frayne, 'The New Majority' (CPS, 2022), esp. pp.55–8.

2 ONS, *Timeseries: United Kingdom Population Mid-Year
   Estimate* (21 December 2022) [https://www.ons.gov.uk/
   peoplepopulationandcommunity/populationandmigration/
   populationestimates/timeseries/ukpop/pop].

3 ONS, *Dataset: Estimates of the Population for the UK, England, Wales,
   Scotland and Northern Ireland* (22 December 2022); ONS, *Births
   in England and Wales: 2022* (17 August 2023). Interestingly, people
   were already worrying about declining birth rates in the 1970s – the
   fertility rate was 1.9, below replacement levels, but still above our
   current 1.6.

4 It is immensely difficult to get perfectly comparable data because
   of the way questions have changed as the population has changed,
   particularly when it comes to those of white but non-British
   backgrounds. We do know now that 82% of our population is white,

but that this includes those with backgrounds from other countries such as in Eastern Europe. See: UK Government, *Ethnicity Facts and Figures* [https://www.ethnicity-facts-figures.service.gov.uk/, accessed 14 February 2024].

5   OECD, *Level of GDP per Capita and Productivity* (USD, constant prices, 2015 PPPs) [https://stats.oecd.org/index.aspx?DataSetCode=PDB_LV, accessed 14 February 2024].

6   Schroders, *What 175 Years of Data Tell Us About House Price Affordability in the UK* (20 February 2023) [https://www.schroders.com/en-gb/uk/individual/insights/what-174-years-of-data-tell-us-about-house-price-affordability-in-the-uk/].

7   To be precise, from 47% to 27%.

8   IFS, *The Rise and Rise of Women's Employment in the UK* (27 April 2018) [https://ifs.org.uk/publications/rise-and-rise-womens-employment-uk].

9   J. Goldthorpe & E. Bukodi, *Social Mobility and Education in Britain* (CUP, 2018).

10 ONS, *Changes in the Economy since the 1970s* (2 September 2019) [https://www.ons.gov.uk/economy/economicoutputandproductivity/output/articles/changesintheeconomysincethe1970s/2019-09-02].

11 World Bank, *Military Expenditure (% of GDP) – United Kingdom* (accessed 13 February 2024). And that 2.2% is based on a more capacious definition of military spending than in 1974.

12 BSA, 'Record number of Brits with no religion', *BSA 34* (NCSR, 2017). See also: The Church of England, *Statistics for Mission 2022* (2023), pp.18–19. On current trends, the Anglican Church will be virtually extinct within two decades.

13 See for example, BSA, 'Homosexuality', *BSA 30* (NCSR, 2013). In 1983 (and by inference in the 1970s), the majority of the population, regardless of party affiliation, considered same-sex relations to be morally wrong.

14 BFI Features, *Britain's Most Watched TV – The 1970s* (22 November 2005) [https://web.archive.org/web/20051122221511/http://www.bfi.org.uk/features/mostwatched/1970s.html].

15 Ipsos, *Issues Index: Trends 1974–1987* [https://www.ipsos.com/en-uk/

issues-index-trends-1974-1987, accessed 14 February 2024]; MORI Social Research Institute, *The More Things Change...: Government, the Economy and Public Services since the 1970s* (October 2003), p.4.

16 YouGov, 'The Most Important Issues Facing the Country', *Trackers* (accessed 11 February 2024). This does not distinguish between legal and illegal migration, but together has them as the third most important issue after health and the economy.

17 Ibid. Although see also: Ipsos, *Ipsos Issues Index January 2024* (10 January 2024), where 31% of people choose health as their top concern. However, in the Ipsos polling, health is bracketed by 'inflation/prices' at 32%, and 'economy' on 31%, where the YouGov poll just has one category for both these issues, 'the economy'. For that and other reasons, the polls are not strictly comparable.

18 And Scottish and Welsh devolution seems to have just replicated the problems of centralisation at a slightly lower level, while introducing a host of new challenges.

19 KCL Policy Institute, *The State of Social Trust: How the UK Compares Internationally* (June 2023) [https://www.kcl.ac.uk/policy-institute/assets/the-state-of-social-trust.pdf].

20 And early evidence suggests it is delivering worse health outcomes for patients. See: K. Williams, 'Is Manchester Great? A New Analysis of NHS Integration' (CPS, 2021).

16 Changing the Climate of Opinion: 10 Years of CapX

1 K. Joseph, *Stranded on the Middle Ground?* (27 October 1976).

2 T. Knox, 'CapX – For Popular Capitalism', *YouTube* (16 June 2014).

3 I. Martin, interviewed by A. Denby.

4 M. Saatchi, interviewed by A. Denby.

5 R. Cunliffe, interviewed by A. Denby.

6 P. Wheatcroft, 'Government has No Place in Takeovers', CapX (19 June 2014); T. Montgomerie, 'Could it be that Boring Conservatism Beats Bold Conservatism?', CapX (19 June 2014).

7 D. Howell, 'Popular Capitalism, Now!', CapX (4 July 2014); G. Warner, 'Is the Pope a Capitalist?', CapX (21 August 2014).

8   J. Clark, 'The Best of the Old and the New: Reissue Classic on the Rise', CapX (16 February 2016).

9   R. Cunliffe, 'Are Cats Libertarians?', CapX (14 March 2015); J. Elsden, 'JRR Tolkien and the Economics of Middle Earth', CapX (1 November 2019).

10 P. Craig, 'Voters were Misled over Brexit – But Mostly by the Remain Campaign', CapX (19 June 2023).

11 R. Colvile, interviewed by A. Denby.

12 R. Colvile, 'What Jeremy Corbyn Really Thinks About Foreign Policy', CapX (13 May 2017); D. Hannan, 'How Can Labour's Leader be in Thrall to Marx?', CapX (1 June 2017).

13 J. Ashmore, interviewed by A. Denby.

14 A. Morton, 'Close the Borders Now – There Won't be a Second Chance', CapX (25 January 2021); A. Denby, 'Boris Must Justify his Long and Winding Roadmap' CapX (23 February 2021).